Riding for Life

A Journey across the North of England

By

Ann Bowes

Illustrations

By

Linda Tindall-Raw

Foreword by Richard Burridge

FRYUP PRESS

First published 2003
By
Fryup Press
Ann@danbymoors.fsnet.co.uk
Whitby, North Yorkshire

ISBN 0-9545951-0-6

Printed in Great Britain
Cromwell Press Ltd, Trowbridge, Wiltshire

To the memory of Dan

Introduction

I never meant to write a book. After I completed my Coast-to Coast ride on Danny-Boy, I only decided to write an account of it as a legacy for my children and grandchildren. As I wrote my story, I found that there was much interest in my account and was encouraged to develop the story into a book.

I hardly knew what I was getting in to and I really don't think I could have accomplished it without the advice and support of some wonderful friends. There is not enough space to thank everyone, but I'd like to record my special appreciation to:

My sister Edna. For her never-ending support and encouragement.

My good friend Joy. For introducing me to computers, with all their pitfalls, and all the subsequent advice and expertise when things inevitably went wrong.

Our dear deceased friend Mick, whose courage, bravery and determination inspired me in all my fundraising efforts for Leukaemia Research.

Brian L. For his knowledge and ability in helping me with the format of my book

Richard. For his great faith in the success of my story and all his subsequent assistance.

....

A share of the profits from this book will be
donated to medical research

Contents

FOREWORD

Having known Ann for a few years, I was happy to lend her my famous horse to help with her cross-country fund-raising ride. Having known Ann for a few years, I would hardly have dared refuse.

After she told me she'd written an account of her ride, I said I'd be happy to look at it. She dropped off a disc and I put off reading it. I was busy, you know how it is.

One night I started reading at about 10pm. I finished after 4am, mesmerised and enchanted. I felt - I still feel - privileged to have read a moving, beguiling story about Yorkshire, about community, about pain and resilience, a story told with great economy and compassion, and so full of affection for all living things that it touched me very deeply.

She paints a picture of England which is both disappearing and still with us, showing us a life on the moors through all its varied seasons. From her poor but idyllic Yorkshire childhood, through the terrible pain of a loss of a child, her spirit shines, making us feel part of something bigger than ourselves.

Enriched by Linda Tindall-Raw's beautiful, evocative illustrations, I believe this is a special book, and a wider public will respond, like me, to its spirited, humble and up-lifting celebration of life and adversity, both ordinary and extraordinary at the same time.

Richard Burridge. North Yorkshire.   August 2003

Part One

CHILDHOOD MEMORIES

Everyone has their dreams. Mine was that I would have a horse of my own and one day we would ride out together on a great adventure.

I suppose my affection for horses began at a very tender age. My earliest memories take me back to the farm where I was born. It was a small, hill farm, situated in a quiet little valley with a stream running through that eventually joined the River Esk. I was the fifth child of seven and my father was still using cart-horses for work on the farm. Tractors had appeared on some farms in the neighbourhood but it was a few years before Dad could afford one.

I must have been only a toddler, not much more than a year old, but I remember Dad carrying me on his shoulders down the pasture in the early morning to bring up Bonny, our cart-horse, ready for work. He would sit me on top of that huge flat back, so soft and warm and I would grasp hold of some of her mane with my chubby little hands while Dad led her back to the stable. She was a dark bay with a big white blaze down her face and huge feet but she was so gentle. I vaguely remember her companion, Blossom, who had passed away. He was a black horse with white markings and when he died my mother wrote a poem. As I grew older, I used to love to read this poem, although it always made me cry - and even today it has the same effect on me. This is the poem my mother wrote:

On our Mare Losing her Mate

Ah dear old horse in grief so dumbly pleading

Bewildered there, you watched where we would go,

And wondered where your team-mate we were leading

His heavy body dragging thro' the snow.

You followed slowly, ponderous, sombre-eyed,

How could you know our faithful friend had died?

And since that day, not really understanding

But with an instinct, making no mistake

You've wandered there; I've watched you sadly standing

Beside his grave. I've felt my own heart ache

But helpless stood and heard you whinny till

The echoes only answered. All was still.

Ah yes, he's gone; in vain you go to find him,

No more he'll pull the wagonload with you

No more he'll canter home with you behind him
We've lost a friend - a trusty one and true
So let him lie, his bed beneath the sky
Old faithful horse, he's said his last goodbye.

I am sure from those first early rides in my life that the seed of 'loving to ride' had been sown. It was to be many years before that seed would grow and flourish.

My childhood years were happy, wild and free. The poverty that existed during those post-war years in so many small farming families like ours had little effect on me. By the time I started school, Bonny had been replaced with a tractor but horses never left my childhood mind. I loved the days when one of our neighbouring farmers, who had a sheep stray adjoining our land, would ride down on his horse to visit Dad. This horse wasn't like the cart-horses we'd had. She was finer built and so shiny and such a beautiful bright bay colour. I used to just stand near her, stroking that lovely smooth coat. I loved the wonderful smell and feel of her and hoped Dad would go on talking all day. If only I could have had a smaller version for myself.

My oldest brother was away at college and both my older sisters were away too, one married and the other at boarding school, but there were still two brothers at home; Mike, who was a few years older and Jimmy, a few years younger than me. We each had our daily jobs to do around the farm like feeding the hens and gathering the eggs. We fed and watered the pigs and bucket-fed the calves with milk.

On Saturdays we cleaned the pig-sty out into a barrow and collected kindling for lighting the fire. One job I loved to do on a summer's evening was to take the sheep dog and go and bring the cows home for milking.

In my spare time, I roamed freely with my brothers. I loved climbing trees and building dams in the beck. We stamped sods of earth off the bank sides with our heels and laid them with stones across the water. When it was hot and sunny, we would take off our socks and shoes and splash about among the rocks and stones. We learned to tickle trout in the streams by lying flat on our tummies and gently reaching down into the cool water below. Sometimes, if we were really quiet, we were lucky enough to catch one and once or twice we managed to get an eel. We always took our successes home and after Dad had cleaned them, Mam would dutifully cook them.

My favourite times were when we went to the woods to collect the kindling, and, having filled our bags, we could then have fun until we thought it was time to go home. We played hide-and-seek and some-times we played cowboys and Indians, making bows and arrows with wood cut from the Hazel trees. I knew how to find the best ones for the arrows without any knots in them. I would run along the sheep-tracks, through bracken and heather, jumping over little gullies and rocks and always riding my pretend pony, happy in my childhood dreams that one day I would have a real pony of my own.

It was only as I grew older and appreciated the value of money that I understood Dad's explanation for his refusal to let me have a pony.

He could keep a cow on the grass and fodder that a pony would eat but it was still a hard fact to face at that young age. I wondered if the day would ever come when I could have a pony. I did have the company of the sheep dogs to enjoy and frequently took one with me on my walks. Sometimes I went alone, looking for birds' nests or watching the trout darting about in the shallow, sunlit pools.

I was never lonely on my own. There was always so much happening all around, rabbits scurrying away down their burrows and hares bounding across the fields. The birds would be singing and calling to each other, occasionally warning calls when they were rearing their young but often just 'happy to be alive' tunes. I learned to recognise the sounds of different birds and one of my favourites was the skylark. I would try and watch it as it soared higher and higher into the sky but I could always hear its song long after it left my sight. Sometimes, if I was lucky, when I walked by the stream where it ran close to the edge of the wood I would see a deer taking a drink. Always alert, it would dart back into the cover of the trees when it saw me.

Time had little meaning for me as I revelled in the wonders of nature. I was often reprimanded for being late, as Mam would soon start to worry and imagine something terrible had happened to me - like falling out of a tree and breaking a leg or slipping in the beck. Mam wasn't country born and saw danger round every corner. I fell head first into a feed barrel one day, cutting my ear along the way. I went into the house with blood streaming down the side of my face, as ears tend to bleed profusely. Poor Mam nearly fainted. She thought I'd split my head open! I still had my jobs to do when I returned home from my walks, even if it was dark, but I was never afraid of the dark, the animals weren't so why should I be?

Dad did eventually let me have a young nanny-goat, which wasn't quite the same as a pony but it was lovely to have something that was just mine. I called her Karen and was allowed to have her because Dad thought she would be useful for rearing pet lambs once she had kidded. I had by now learnt to hand-milk the cows and quite enjoyed milking my goat. I didn't need a milking stool to sit on when I milked Karen. I would just give her some kositos in a scoop out in the stack-yard and then I would sit on the grass next to her with my pail. She stood very still and never kicked like some of the cows did. She was a real pet and followed me around everywhere when I let her off her tethering rope. She was a bit mischievous, too, and liked to pull the washing off the line, so I had to tie her up on washing-days. When she started following me right into the house she wasn't allowed off her rope any more.

I have only happy memories of those years and I lived wild and free in the beautiful countryside around our farm.

A DREAM COME TRUE

When I was eleven, my life changed. I passed my eleven-plus examination, which qualified me for a place in a convent boarding school. It was a complete shock to me, leaving home, and those happy, carefree days of my childhood never returned. I made many friends during my five years at the convent and the schooling itself was bearable but I hated the long hours of confinement. The house rules were very strict and we weren't allowed off the premises. Everyone was in bed and lights out by nine o'clock. I was often homesick and really missed my brothers, my home and all the animals.

My favourite lessons were music, maths and P.E. I loved to sing and was delighted when I was accepted into both the boarders' and the school choirs. I enjoyed all the sports we played and represented my school at netball. Gym was a great favourite too, and my ability to climb trees came in useful as I quickly learned to climb the ropes in the sports hall. My teacher was so impressed that I had to demonstrate to the whole class how it was done.

Some of the girls, whose parents were obviously quite well off, went to a local riding school in the town on Saturday mornings for lessons. How I envied them, all dressed up in their smart cream jodhpurs and yellow, polo neck sweaters. It was the first time I had ever seen real riding hats and long, black, riding boots. One day, I told myself, I would have some just like theirs.

I found the summer evenings the hardest to cope with. Being kept inside so much made me feel like a caged animal. I longed for the holidays when I could go home to the wide, open spaces and the sights and smells of the farm and the freedom to go where I wanted. My goat had been sold when I went away to school but I still loved to be back home, helping Dad with the milking and all the other many jobs on the farm. It was great to be back with my brothers, teasing them, playing football or cricket and going rabbiting, when I always had to carry the bag of nets for them. They didn't trust me to carry the ferrets. We still went down to the beck to catch trout and the occasional eel.

After I left school, I took a job in a Post-Office and village store in Rosedale. It was here that I met my husband to be, Allan, and he introduced me to a farmer friend of his. I became friends with this farmer and his family, as he often gave me a lift to church on Sundays.

He and his wife had three young daughters for whom they'd bought a pony. When he became aware how much I longed to ride, I was invited to take the pony out. Although I stressed to him that I couldn't ride, he insisted that I'd be fine and sent me on my way.

Misty, as her name implied, was a stocky little grey, of Welsh extraction, standing about 13. 2. hands. Feeling very excited, I set off from the farm on the road leading down the valley. Although a little apprehensive, I felt elated and ecstatically happy. Could this really be happening? Here I was on a pony, riding out on my own.

It took me a while to get used to the movement in the saddle and when we trotted I'm sure I wasn't doing it as I should have been but I just loved it. After we'd climbed up the steep Chimney bank and turned off on to the old disused railway line, I managed, with some energetic kicking of my heels, to persuade Misty to go into a canter. This was much easier and we galloped along the gravelly track, the whole of the dale spread out before us, until Misty decided she needed a rest. At the top of the dale I managed to find the track leading back down to the fields and, after negotiating a few gates, arrived back at the farm in one piece. Hot and sweaty and covered with horse-hair, I had just enjoyed two of the best hours of my life.

I was still only eighteen when Allan and I were married, and, a year later I gave birth to a beautiful baby girl, whom we called Sara. The following year, shortly after the birth of our second child, Michael, Allan was offered a job as a gamekeeper. This had been his ambition for a while and delightedly he accepted, and we moved to

Wensleydale with our two babies. I loved being a mother, caring for my little ones, and horses were temporarily pushed to the back of my mind. A third child arrived, Danny, a brother for Sara and Mike, keeping my life very busy. We lived near the edge of the moor, which I loved and I spent many happy hours with my young family.

Allan knew of my love of horses and had promised me that if ever we were lucky enough to be where we had any land, I would have my horse. Sara was four when Allan was offered the job where we now live. This meant that we would be living back nearer to both our families, which was great but better still, there was a field adjoining the house for our own use. A field of three acres! My heart skipped a beat - that meant I would be able to have my horse. What joy! I could barely wait for the weeks to pass when we would be moving to our new home.

After we were settled into our new house, I started to hunt through the 'horses for sale' columns in the papers, hoping to find one we could afford. The horse we eventually chose was a large black cob that had been used for pulling a rag-and-bone cart in the towns. He was very quiet and gentle and we decided to call him Napoleon but afterwards he was always known as 'Nap'. We knew he would be good in traffic, due to his previous work, but he hadn't been ridden very much. He was delivered to our house late one evening and I was so excited I couldn't wait to sit on him. I had no saddle or bridle but I just had to get on him. I couldn't believe that after all these years I really had a horse of my own. The sound of the wagon could still be

heard going back down the hill when, leaving Allan looking on with our three little ones, I led my horse proudly from the stable into the field. With only a rope attached to his head-collar, I took hold of his long black mane and jumped up on to his broad back and off we went up the field. At last, a horse of my own - I was in heaven!

I was determined to ride well, studying many books from the library and working hard practising my skills. There wasn't a lot of free time for riding, and three years later I had another baby, David, completing my family. As the years passed, my riding improved and I progressed to other horses. I bought in youngsters, schooled and trained them and then sold them on. Eventually, I broke horses in, always trying to learn more about them and continuing to read how to work and school them. No two horses are alike. They all have their own individual character and I learned from all of them as they learned from me. One day, I hoped I might breed one of my own.

When the children were old enough, I taught each of them to ride and, after much persuasion, I even managed to teach Allan. It took him several lessons to master the rising trot. He went to great lengths to explain to me how much easier it was for women. It could, he said, be extremely painful for men if they didn't do it exactly right. He did eventually become quite a proficient rider and in the months that followed, we used to have a good laugh about his learning experiences.

The love of freedom and wild places was always with me and now I could enjoy these things with my horses. I became familiar with all the tracks and bridleways in this beautiful part of Yorkshire by the Esk valley. I loved riding through the hills and galloping over the moors, feeling the cold wind or the gentle rain on my face. Every season has its own special delights, the wonderful fragrance of blossom on the trees in Springtime, the pungent smell of bluebells carpeting the earth in June, the rich swathes of purple blanketing the moors in late Summer, with its intoxicating honeyed perfume.

I thrilled to the calls of the birds, each recognisable by its own individual sound as I rode quietly through tree-lined tracks beneath the craggy rock faces. I once came across two fox-cubs in a clearing among the trees. I stood my horse still as I sat and watched them playing in the sunshine. Unafraid of the horse, they were completely unaware of the silent onlooker sitting quietly watching their antics. When I am riding up on the moors, I feel at peace with the world. When problems or stresses enter my life, I find the best remedy is to saddle up my horse and go for a ride. The tranquillity and vastness of the moors seem to put life back into perspective.

If only a remedy for the problems of life could always be so simple - but life is never easy, as I was to realise only too soon.

TEARS OF SADNESS, TEARS OF JOY

When my youngest son left school and started work, I felt a sense of hopelessness and sadness that was difficult to explain. It was as if I had been made redundant. I was still a housewife, running a home and taking care of my family, I had a part-time job as a waitress, worked hard in my garden and looked after the kennels for Allan's dogs, but I no longer felt needed in the same way. I thought long and hard and wondered what to do. One of my older sisters suggested I think of something where I would feel really needed. Maybe charity work, or something to do with horses.

In the days that followed, I thought of something. About twenty miles away there was a school that catered for disabled children, and I knew they gave riding lessons to their pupils. Maybe that's what I could do. I had   received so much pleasure from horses, and now I could help children less fortunate than me to have that pleasure too.

I rang the school and was invited along to their next riding lesson. The group was a member of the Riding for the Disabled Association (R.D.A.) so it had a qualified physiotherapist and riding instructor, but they still needed helpers. One person was needed to lead the pony and one to walk either side to aid and support the child.

I will never forget the look on the face of one little girl, who was wheelchair bound, the day she actually sat on a pony for the very first time. She had overcome great fear and apprehension but her smile of sheer joy and disbelief brought tears to my eyes. She was now just like any normal child and it wasn't important that her legs didn't work

properly. She didn't need them when she was riding. She was lifted off at the end of her lesson, bursting with pride, saying that her parents would never believe what she had just done. That little girl continued her lessons and became a confident young rider, learning to trot and control her pony with the limited use she had in her arms. I felt privileged to have been her helper. There were many other such children and doing this work each week helped fill a need in me.

This branch of the R.D.A. was independent from the school and had to fund itself, so they constantly needed to raise money. I wanted to help with this and so, at our next fund-raising meeting, I agreed to hold a coffee evening in my garden. I had held similar events before, dances and domino drives in the village hall to raise money for clubs connected with my children, like the tennis and cricket clubs. The coffee evening went very well. It was a beautiful summer evening and as the sun went down it cast long clear shadows across the hills in the dale head. Many of my new friends from the riding school came to support me, as well as local people, and it was a great success. Raising money for the R.D.A. was different from what I had done in the past and gave me a warm feeling inside. I continued to support them for many years.

In the spring of 1993 I discussed with Allan the possibility of putting my mare in foal. Ruby, as she was called, was a super little horse - a chestnut thoroughbred, very intelligent and gentle. She was only 15. 1.hands but had loads of stamina and was lovely to ride. We had bought her six years earlier and soon discovered that she had in the past been terribly ill treated. She was terrified of being tied up and could not be caught out in the field. It took me several months of kindness and patience before she would stand quietly stalled in the stable without trying frantically to break free. She never did accept being tied up outside, all the years that I had her.

She was now twelve years old, and to my delight Allan agreed to the mating, so we asked around, trying to find a suitable stallion. We finally decided on an Irish Draught/Thoroughbred cross and arrangements were made. When the time was right for Ruby, we loaded her into the trailer and off we went, hopes held high. Everything went smoothly, and I was very excited at the prospect of breeding my own foal in eleven months time.

In May of the following year, when Ruby was close to foaling, something happened which was to have a lasting effect on all our lives. Our second son Dan, then aged 25, was tragically drowned. The pain was unbearable and Allan was inconsolable. Sara, now married with two children of her own, and the two other lads were deeply affected, suffering greatly for a long time. In my own deep grief I had to try and comfort each of them. For myself, it felt as though a part of me had been torn away from within, leaving a great empty wound inside that would never heal. Sometimes the pain was so intense I wished that I would not wake up the next day. I don't know how I lived through those terrible black days. Life could never be the same again.

Dan built dry-stone walls and was well known and liked in the hamlets and villages in our valley. He had inherited the great love and understanding of the countryside that Allan and I shared. He had roamed the hills and valleys since he'd been a little boy, always with a dog as his companion. Everyone he met was greeted with friendliness and a big happy smile.

He was drowned in a terrible accident one night when his car was washed over a newly built high-level ford. Heavy rain had flooded the river causing the water to rise rapidly. In later weeks, after many protestations from local people, a safety barrier was built on the downstream side of the ford, to prevent such an accident ever happening again. The pain was immense and for a time life had little meaning. It was just the support and comfort from friends and family that helped us through those dark days. They all shared with us the heavy burden of pain.

There was just one ray of sunshine in all my darkness. Three weeks after we lost Dan, Ruby gave birth to a beautiful, healthy, colt foal. I was awakened one night by frantic whinnying. I had checked on Ruby at two in the morning and she'd been grazing contentedly. I hurriedly pulled on some clothes and ran outside into the field. There, as dawn was breaking, sitting all alone, seemingly without a care in the world, was this handsome, chestnut foal. Tears of joy filled my eyes as I beheld the marvellous sight. I was overcome with awe that the miracle of new birth brings.

As I ran across the field, I could make out the form of Ruby in the next field, running up and down behind the wall. I could only assume that she had been terrified by the afterbirth, swinging behind her as it came away and in fleeing from it had jumped the wall. The reason for the frantic calling was that she didn't know how to get back again to her newborn baby. I ran to the hand gate to let her through.

My joy turned to horror, when I saw in the breaking light of day, blood oozing from a deep wound in her chest. As she rushed past me towards her baby, I noticed blood on all her legs.

Once inside, with a better light, we could see the true extent of her injuries. The chest wound looked deep and there were several tears and cuts on all four legs. The worst of these was on her near foreleg. Ruby herself seemed unperturbed and was gently licking and nuzzling her newborn, all the time nickering softly to him. The foal did not seem to be having much success, and knowing how important the first milk is to any newborn, I decided to call my neighbour John, who runs a stud farm.

When John arrived he was horrified at the state Ruby was in, but his main concern was for the foal. Fortunately, one of his Cleveland Bay mares had foaled a day earlier and, hoping her milk would still contain enough of the antibodies vital to any newborn animal, he rushed back home. He soon returned with a full bottle and while Allan held the foal, John succeeded in getting half of the milk down the little fellow. In the meantime, as is nature's way, the foal would continue to suckle his mother, which would encourage the milk to flow. After what seemed like an age the vet arrived and injected the injured leg with an anaesthetic. After examining my foal, he declared that he was a grand little fellow and in perfect health. He then tended all Ruby's wounds and gave her a long lasting antibiotic injection.

By the next day, Ruby had come to her milk and two days later, with her foal, I turned her back out into the field. Apart from being stiff and sore, there was hopefully no lasting damage. Each day I brought her in to the stable and tended her wounds, which slowly began to heal.

Since the tragedy of Dan, there had been one name in my mind for the unborn foal. We called him Danny-Boy. He brought new life and a reason to live. To help combat the pain of my grief and face up to the future, I threw myself into my charity work and started to organise an Open Garden Day. It was to be the first of many such days.

THE GROWING

YEARS

Over the next three years Danny-Boy grew into a fine looking youngster. He was a very friendly fellow, always playful and he loved to be with you. He was led about on a lead rein when just a few weeks old, first following behind his mother and later on his own. When Danny-Boy was three months old, I started riding Ruby again. Her wounds had all mended and even the scar on the front leg was slowly fading. It was good to be back in the saddle and she didn't mind too much having to leave her baby behind. Danny-Boy soon got used to Ruby being away and gradually I was able to increase the length of time when he was left alone.

When Ruby and I were returning from our rides, about half a mile from home Ruby would call out to Danny-Boy, as if to say, 'I'm back' and there was always an answering high-pitched whinnying in reply. After I'd unsaddled Ruby and turned her loose in the field, it amused me to watch Danny-Boy showing his delight at her return by bucking and dancing around her, before searching for a comforting suckle of milk. Ruby nickered softly to him while gently nuzzling him in a reassuring way. She was a good, protective mother and I was filled with pride as I watched them both canter across the field, their rich chestnut coats shining in the bright sunlight. The pleasure I experienced watching Danny-Boy in those early weeks helped ease a little of the pain and sadness felt deep in my heart since our tragic loss.

As the days grew shorter and the leaves began to fall from the trees, I began to wean Danny-Boy off his mother. Ruby was brought into her stable for the winter and for the next couple of weeks he only suckled twice a day. Gradually, he was weaned off her altogether and I now provided all the food and drink that he needed. He soon recognised my voice and shouted a welcome to me each morning. Over Winter he lost his baby coat and to my delight, when his new coat grew through, it was a lovely bay colour. The following spring I had him gelded, and he continued to grow strong and healthy.

Two years later I started the serious task of breaking him in. The three months I spent working with him on the lunge and long reins passed quickly, and the day arrived for me to ride him for the first time.

There had been few setbacks and nothing seemed to bother him too much, and I spoke softly to him, stroking and patting him regularly, reassuring him and only raising my voice when correcting him.

On the morning I was to ride him, I tacked him up as usual but left the head-collar on underneath the bridle and led him round into the paddock. Allan had agreed to help me and was holding the lead rein attached to the head-collar, while I gathered the reins loosely, put my left foot into the stirrup, pulled myself up and gently lowered my weight into the saddle. I sat awhile, talking quietly and patting him before taking up the reins and asking Allan to lead him slowly forwards. For a few yards all went well but then Danny-Boy got a little excited and wanted to charge off. Allan held on to his lead rope and we waited until he settled down before starting again. This time he seemed more relaxed as we continued walking him round, and although Allan was still holding the lead rope, I now began to use the reins to ask Danny-Boy to change direction. He responded well to all I asked of him and after ten minutes I drew him to a halt. Delighted with his performance, I praised him warmly, patting him on his neck before taking my feet out of the stirrups and gently sliding to the ground.

I was bursting with happiness as I led him back to the stable. I had longed for this day since he was a foal, watching him grow into adulthood, and I hadn't been disappointed. I rode him most days that summer, continuing his training. Things didn't always go according to plan but he was always such a happy horse and a delight to ride. I tried to teach him something new each time we rode out; training him was not only rewarding but gave me immense pleasure. During the following months he learned to trust me and our confidence in each other grew.

During these years I continued to hold my Charity events and my Open Garden days had continued to prosper. I grew plants, baked cakes and made lots of jam, all to sell on the appropriate stalls. Friends and neighbours came to help me, bringing more produce for the stalls and we sold tea and scones, ice cream and soft drinks. There were pony-rides, a bouncy castle and organised games for the children.

My husband's work brought him into contact with many people, one of whom was Richard Burridge, the owner of the famous racehorse, Desert Orchid. This particular year, I contacted Richard and told him all about my Garden Day. I asked him if there was any chance of Desert Orchid making a guest appearance. His reply was very positive and I had explained to Richard that I was raising money for Leukaemia Research, and knew he would be sympathetic as he had recently lost his mother from cancer.

Leukaemia Research was very close to my heart. Around the time we lost Dan, a great friend of ours, Mick, was diagnosed with this terrible disease. He was undergoing treatment but still managed to continue riding when he felt well enough. I did some research and realised how many people leukaemia affected, especially children. Much to my delight, Richard was able to bring 'Dessie' along to my Garden Day. The weather turned out beautiful with bright sunshine and lots of people, and the day was a huge success.

AN IDEA IS
CONCEIVED

It was in the autumn of Danny-Boy's fifth year that I had my big idea. 'Next year, why not do a sponsored horse-ride instead of a garden day?' The idea kept growing in my head. 'How about a coast-to-coast ride? Was I up to that?' At fifty-four I wasn't exactly young, but I was fit and healthy and I had a good horse.

I was sure Danny-Boy would love it, he was a fine strong horse now, standing at sixteen hands. He still had his boyish nature and people often commented on what a happy horse he seemed but he was mature enough when it came to work. We had developed a great confidence in each other. He learned quickly, and loved the moors as much as I did, always sure-footed along the steep, stony tracks. He loved splashing through the streams and rivers, and wasn't afraid to-push past low branches in the narrow forest tracks. His trust in me told him I would never ask anything of which he was not capable.

The more I thought about doing a sponsored horse ride, the more excited I became. I knew a girl, Bridget, who had completed a coast-to-coast ride some years before. She had since married and I didn't know her married name, but I was able to get her number from her parents. When I called she was busy, but very interested, and invited me over later that day. I couldn't concentrate on anything while I waited to go - filled with anticipation, I drove the nine miles over the moors to her house.

Over a cup of coffee, she explained what was involved - detailed routes, a back-up team, a riding companion, places to stay and a lot of organisation. Bridget showed me the scrapbook of her ride, and I felt the excitement rising by the minute. She had found it strenuous but very enjoyable, and said she'd love to come along as my companion, if I ever got the ride organised

All the way home my mind was racing. I didn't know how Allan would react. He was normally very supportive of my charity functions, allowing me to get on with them, and helping out on the day. This was something quite different. After dinner I broached the subject. He was not in the least surprised and reacted with complete indifference. He thought it wouldn't really be possible and that I would be taking on too much, but didn't dampen my enthusiasm. He probably thought it was the last he would hear of it, but my heart was set. This didn't have to be a dream. I could make it happen.

The next day, I decided to take Danny-Boy out to think things over properly. There had been a slight frost but not enough to make it dangerous and after doing my jobs I saddled up Danny-Boy and set off down the road leading to the dale head.

The rising sun had melted the hoar frost from the fields, leaving only the whitened strip behind each wall where its rays had not yet reached. The sky was clear and blue with only a few wisps of cloud to the west, daring to remain. There was a smell of autumn in the air and the leaves were already losing their rich green shades of summer.

As I rode up the valley, I noticed the ripened fruit of the elderberry hanging in clusters of shiny black berries much loved by all the birds for winter food. The holly berries, too, were already changing from green to the more noticeable bright red. It made me think of Christmas when I was a child, for our Christmas tree was always cut from a holly tree. For years I never knew that a real Christmas tree was something quite different.

I eventually left the hard road and turned through a hand-gate, taking a track that led up the steep bank side. Here the bracken was already a golden brown, except in a few sheltered places and it snapped crisply under Danny-Boy's feet where it lay across the path. As we climbed higher, the path became steeper with stones and deep ruts that had been formed where the storms and rain had washed away the earth. Danny-Boy picked his way up the hillside, carefully avoiding the soft, boggy patches and protruding rocks and stones. We arrived at the top where another gate led us through to the open moor.

As I turned to close the gate, I looked back down the valley and gazed in wonder. Far below, further down the dale, a sea of mist lay like a white blanket, the distant hills rising from it like islands in an ocean. The mist had crept slowly up the valleys from the sea during the night and only the rising sun had prevented it from reaching the entire length of the valley. Now, the morning sun was hastening its retreat.

I felt in awe at this wonderful sight. Even as I sat watching, the sea of mist was slowly receding, exposing more and more of the surrounding hills. The magical moment passed as Danny-Boy tossed his head, impatient to continue. I patted him in appreciation of his patience with me and set off up the moorland track through the heather. The air was cooler here and the thin layers of ice on the puddles splintered like glass under Danny-Boy's feet.

As we trotted along the pathway, a flock of fieldfares flew over us, their noisy chatter short-lived as they were soon out of sight. Many flocks pass over the moors in October, stopping temporarily to feed, as they journey south on their long trip from Scandinavia. Occasionally, we see small groups of snow buntings too, stopping to feed and rest awhile as they also make their way south. Many of these birds travel from as far north as the Arctic Circle.

The moors are much quieter now that the summer is over. The curlews, peewits and golden plovers that come to nest and raise their young on the moors have long gone back to the river estuaries and coastal regions for the winter. Only the grouse stay with us all the year round, the heather being both their food and their home.

When we reached a good stretch of track, I urged Danny-Boy into a canter. The cold air stung my nostrils and made my eyes water. I felt at one with him as we galloped along, jumping over little streams that crossed the track and side-stepping the large rocks. The only sound being the rhythmic drumming of hooves on the hard earth and occasional clang of metal as his shoes caught the small stones and pebbles.

Suddenly I heard a strange sound above me and pulled Danny-Boy back to a walk. Looking up I saw high in the sky the familiar vee formation of a flock of migrating geese. Now I knew winter was really on its way. The Brent geese leave their breeding grounds in Northern Siberia and fly south to all parts of North-Western Europe. Those that we see settle in the estuaries of Eastern and Southern England. They fly in vee formation as each bird benefits from the air current created by the one flying in front of it. The leading bird is usually a very strong, experienced female who will occasionally be relieved of her position by an equally strong flyer. They were soon gone from my sight and I continued my ride.

Soon we left the main track and turned down a little used bridleway. The path is not easy to follow and after heavy rains becomes very soft and boggy. I had to steer Danny-Boy round some of the worst places because the peaty soil makes them treacherous. Unsuspecting riders could soon find themselves in difficulty. With only the sheep as my witness, I didn't want to find myself stuck in a peat bog. I didn't think that the sheep would come to my rescue.

We were soon over the worst places and the going became sound and firm once more. I let Danny-Boy pick his own way and looking round the moor, I spotted, flying low over rushes, (or seves as they're known locally) the laboured flight of a short-eared owl. It looked like a giant moth as it flapped along, no more than two feet above the ground, searching for its favourite food. Perhaps 'short-sighted' would have been a more apt name. It is known locally as the 'bog' owl because of the terrain in which it hunts, searching for its staple diet of voles. It makes no sound and is one of the few members of the owl family that hunts in daylight.

Presently we reached the road again, and turning eastwards towards home, made our way back down the ridge. As I reached the top of the hill leading down into the dale, I had the most spectacular view. I could see the distant moors on the far side of the Esk valley, and further still, the farms stretching towards the cliff tops above the North Sea. Today the sea was as blue as the sky, and I could even make out a couple of trawlers heading back to port with their night's catch. The fishermen must appreciate such wonderful calm conditions for they are few and far between in the autumn.

Trotting down the road towards home, my thoughts returned to my envisaged journey across the country. Maybe it was just the wonderful day or the ride I'd had with Danny-Boy. Maybe it was just the privileged feeling I felt at being able to enjoy the beautiful world around me, but whatever it was, I now knew I had to try and attempt that ride. I knew it would be hard work, but the rewards I was sure, would make it all worthwhile.

PLANNING THE ROUTE

Over the next few weeks I tried to find out as much information as possible. I got in touch with different horse societies, long-distance riders and people connected with the upkeep of bridleways. I began to realise that the best way of organising such a ride was to devise a route of my own, so I turned to a map of northern England. Working westwards from Fryup, where we lived, I studied it to see if I had any contacts who might be able to accommodate me.

I had friends with horses at Helmsley whom I was sure would be interested in helping. I met Dawne through my work with the R. D.A. and we had remained good friends. Further west at Kirby-Wiske, I had an old school pal, Mary, with whom I'd kept in touch over the years, who lived on a farm. Mary had been through hard times. She hadn't been married many years when her husband was tragically killed in a road accident, leaving her to bring up their two small children on her own. She also had to take her husband's place on his parents' farm. Being the tough, determined character that she is, she succeeded admirably and now life was easier as her children were grown up and had successful careers. When I contacted Mary on the phone, her response was what I expected. She was full of enthusiasm and wanted to help in any way she could. I promised to keep her informed if my plans succeeded.

Studying the map again, I thought perhaps friends in Wensleydale might also be able to help. Laurie, an old childhood friend of Allan's, and his wife Linda had also experienced much sadness in their lives. They, too, had lost a son in his early twenties two years before we lost Dan. Another son had been diagnosed with a form of leukaemia and had undergone several courses of treatment. This had proved successful and Andrew was now married with a baby boy, Daniel, and was doing fine. Linda was also involved in charity fund-raising so I felt sure that she and Laurie would want to assist me. But there was still a lot of country to cross between their home and the west coast. I was going to need more contacts.

A couple of weeks later, Laurie called in to see us. I was delighted to see him - just the person I needed to talk to. I told him all about my ride and, knowing each other as we did, he wasn't a bit surprised but laughingly said I was 'a very ambitious lady'. Staying with them was no problem and he was curious to know my route. With the map laid out before us I told him what I'd sorted out so far, and he suggested I plan a route from the nearest coastal region to their house. I wouldn't need to travel all the way from the far side of the Lake District, as I'd first thought, as I would still be riding from coast to coast. We decided that Morecambe Bay would be ideal. I would still be travelling from coast to coast, finishing at Runswick Bay.

Studying the map further, we worked out that it would take seven consecutive days of riding and so I still needed two more places to stay. Laurie had a black fell pony, Darkie, and used him to pull a landau for weddings. He also rode Darkie, so knew the country around his home very well and agreed to map out that part of my route with me. He added that, if I ever got this project off the ground, he might ride with me on the day I would be in his area. This was great news. Laurie also thought he might be able to find accommodation for us a day's ride from his house. This meant I would only need one more place to break the journey from there to the coast.

Things were beginning to take shape and I went about my daily chores with new vigour, all the time thinking and planning and, above all, hoping that my dream would be possible. My rides with Danny-Boy took on more significance and I had to think about his training as I couldn't afford anything to happen to him now.

I returned to my map to study the western region of my route and the name Bentham rang a bell in my head. Surely, that was where my cousin Pete and his family lived, and Bentham looked about a day's ride from the coast. Pete was quite a few years younger than me but we knew each other well, as years ago he used to stay on our farm during the school holidays. He was impressed and enthusiastic about my ride, asking how he could help. I said I needed accommodation for myself and for two horses, and he had to think hard. He had no land with his property, and with three children had no spare rooms either. He thought it best to advertise in his local parish magazine. The days passed and I was impatient to hear from him.

In the meantime, I realised that I would need someone to ride with me. This would be much more enjoyable for me and Danny-Boy, as horses love company too. I thought of Maggie, a friend who lived with her husband and family on a farm in Rosedale, a few miles over the moors. Three years earlier I had taught Maggie to ride on Allan's horse, Cammy. Maggie is a vivacious redhead whose infectious laughter is instantly recognisable and we had enjoyed many great rides together over the moors. I eventually sold Cammy to her and she went on to do long-distance riding whenever time allowed. Although Cammy was now eighteen, the Arab in her made up for her lack of youth and she was still a good horse.

I rang Maggie and asked her if she would like to come with me as my companion. She was thrilled and flattered that I thought she was up to such a ride, the excitement evident in her voice. She said how wonderful it would be but she had doubts about whether she could get away for a whole week. I told Maggie to discuss it with her husband Chris, letting me know as soon as she could. I knew things would be difficult for her as she did a lot of work on the farm, as well as doing all the farm accounts and looking after their three school-age children. But knowing Maggie as I did, I knew if there was half a chance of her coming, she'd take it!

Sometime before Christmas, now convinced in my own mind that I was really going to attempt this ride, I contacted Kathy Gale. Kathy is chairman of the Cleveland and Middlesbrough branch of the Leukaemia Research Fund, whom I knew well from my previous fund raising efforts. She was delighted to hear about my venture and offered her support and assistance

Christmas was fast approaching and I was very busy with family preparations and organising our Christmas 'Songs of Praise'. This is a charity concert held in our village hall and performed by the choir of which I am choir mistress. Realising I was going to need help orga-nizing my ride, I asked Carol, a fellow choir-member and friend, with secretarial skills, if she would be willing to help. She happily agreed. Next, I spoke to Ian, a neighbour down the road, asking him if he would help to co-ordinate all the details of the ride. He was glad to be involved, too. I told them both we would start in earnest in the New Year .

MAPS, MEETINGS AND MISSIVES

Some things happen in life when you least expect them. Allan and I had been to visit my aunt in Harrogate on Boxing Day and while we were travelling home the following day, I knew that I was sickening for something. Feeling worse with each passing mile, I barely had the strength to crawl into bed when we arrived back at Fryup. By then I realised that I had gone down with a particularly nasty strain of flu. After three days I managed to get up but was still feeling very groggy and weak. Allan was having to do most of my chores as well as feeding and exercising all the dogs when he returned home from work each day. He had also been looking after Danny-Boy for me, turning him out in the field each day with his rug on, for his exercise.

On the Saturday morning he came in from doing his jobs, saying he thought he would like to take Danny-Boy for a ride. I was delighted but very surprised, as Allan had not ridden for quite a few years. As I was beginning to feel better I went outside to see them off. It was good to see Allan back in the saddle. The week looking after Danny-Boy had given Allan renewed confidence to ride again.

My plans had been delayed because of my illness, but later in the month I decided I was well enough to get things under-way again and organise a meeting. I contacted Ian and Carol to arrange a suitable evening for them to come to our house. Kathy was also able to join us and brought a large box of headed note-paper, sponsor-sheets, blank headed posters and stickers for collecting boxes. We sat pooling our thoughts, discussing ideas and making lists of all the people and places where I would eventually deliver the sponsor sheets.

We also drafted letters asking people to sponsor my ride. These were put into three categories. People who knew me, people who didn't know me but had businesses in our locality, and associates of Allan's who came shooting grouse on the moors. We were all given jobs to do. Ian was going to make lists of radio stations and newspapers that covered the route. Carol would type as many letters as possible to potential sponsors and I was to deliver the sponsor sheets. Before the next meeting, we were each to think of ways to publicise the ride. We finished with a well-earned glass of wine, happy with how things had gone.

We'd also decided we needed a poster showing the planned route and a photograph of me on Danny-Boy, so I approached another neighbour, Brian, who kindly agreed to come and take the photograph and design the poster. Brian always designed and printed the posters for my Garden Days, Charity Concerts and any other event I was organising. This was always his donation and, creating them gave him a welcome break from his very stressful work at the hospital.

Brian arrived the following Sunday morning to take the pictures and we were blessed with beautiful weather. He promised to deliver the posters within a few days. I felt I was making real progress.

The day after our meeting, I telephoned Maggie and we had a long chat about my ride. She was now very determined to come with me but was concerned that Cammy might not be up to such a rigorous journey, and didn't want to let me down. She decided to have Cammy examined by a vet. I pointed out that it wasn't imperative for her to complete the entire ride, as people were sponsoring *me*. She felt much happier on hearing this and promised to keep me informed when she had any news.

The next time I went shopping, I bought all the ordnance survey maps covering the areas of my planned route and photocopied and enlarged the relevant sections. My next task would be to check every mile of the route and find out where it was possible to use bridleways. Not a job to be completed in one day!

The following week my cousin Pete rang with good news. He had received a reply from his advert from some neighbours offering to let us graze our horses in their field, and had arranged for us to visit them the following Sunday. Now the route was taking shape but I still needed another stopover between Bentham and Wensleydale.

Later that same week, I had a visitor. Tanya was a location manager on 'Heartbeat', which is filmed in our area, and had earlier asked about using our house and kennels for a scene. It proved to be not quite what they were looking for, but I enjoyed meeting her and discussing her work.

After Tanya had finished taking photographs, I told her about my ride. I was hoping she might have some contacts that could help with the publicity. I began to give her details about the route and when I mentioned Morecambe Bay, her face lit up. I couldn't believe it when she said she had once lived there and had been to the local school!

Tanya described the small town of Bolton-le-Sands and the surrounding area, including a parking strip very close to the coast where we would be able to unbox the horses. She even drew a sketch showing the access lane leading down on to the shoreline where we would find the hard-standing area. She added names, railway lines, caravan sites and traffic lights. I couldn't believe my good fortune. Tanya was glad that she had been able to help and wished me all the luck in the world. I knew I would need it. I waved her goodbye with a huge smile on my face.

A TRIP TO

MORECAMBE BAY

I had by now convinced Allan of my determination to attempt this ride - and also persuaded him to take a week's holiday, which he rarely took, and come with me to drive the Land Rover and trailer. I knew that he would have a busy week but felt sure he would enjoy it. It was a great relief to know he would be around and I was very happy to think we were embarking on this adventure together.

On the Sunday, Allan and I set off across the country to Bentham to see my cousin Pete, so we could meet the couple who had volunteered to let Danny-Boy and Cammy stay with them. We had never visited this area before but, following Pete's instructions, we found his house without too much difficulty. When we arrived it was pouring with rain and Pete telephoned the couple, David and Marie, to inform them of our impending visit. Pete apologised for not being able to come with us but following his instructions, we found their home and on arriving, were greeted warmly and invited in to their house.

Marie explained how they could help Their land was divided into three small paddocks and they had stabling where their ponies were brought in each evening. We could turn our horses into the bottom paddock and Marie would then be able to turn her ponies out again after we had left each day. We could use the top paddock for a parking area for the vehicles. After we had been outside and looked around we agreed it would be an excellent arrangement.

We returned to the house and I questioned David about the best route from Bolton-le-Sands to Bentham. We studied the map but no one was familiar with any bridleways beyond Bentham. David did advise us on the best route to take over to the coast by road, and telephoned an acquaintance on a British Bridleways committee. I made notes and was grateful to Marie for finding me the telephone numbers of her blacksmith and vet in case either horse lost a shoe or suffered an injury.

Allan and I had previously decided it would be better to travel over to Bentham on the Sunday of the week of the ride, then travel the short distance to the coast on the Monday morning. This would give the horses time to recover from standing in the trailer for over four hours.

After a welcome cup of tea, Marie invited us all to stay with them the first two nights of the ride and save on our expenses. Allan and I were most appreciative, and promised to keep them informed about my plans before we left to continue our journey to Morecambe Bay.

We passed through many villages, crossed over the M.6, drove on through more villages before arriving in Bolton-le-Sands and we finally made it to the edge of the bay. We found the hard standing exactly as described by Tanya. The sea itself seemed far away with grass and mudflats leading down to the water's edge. It had stopped raining but the sky was dull and threatening with a cool breeze blowing in from the sea. Some sheep were grazing near by, trying to find sustenance from the stunted vegetation.

We drove back into town and found somewhere to eat before retracing our tracks to Bentham and on to Ingleton. While Allan was driving, I was making notes and trying to memorise names and places. In Ingleton, we took the route by the river, and then climbed up the road leading into Chapel-le-Dale. This would be the route we would be taking with the horses, well away from the main road carrying all the heavy traffic. This was an access road for the many scattered farms up this side of the valley. A stone wall ran the full length of the valley to our right and on our left was a narrow strip of sheep pasture rising to the foot of the high limestone cliffs. High above, the jagged outcrops of rock were etched starkly against the skyline. Across the valley on our right, we could just make out the imposing heights of Ingleborough towering over the Pennines.

I could feel the excitement welling up inside me, longing for the day I would be here with Danny-Boy. How I would enjoy those wonderful views and the atmosphere of those bleak moors and fells. My skin tingled just thinking about it. I felt the day would not come soon enough. We rejoined the main road to Hawes and made our way back home to Fryup. We arrived late but happy, knowing that our day had been successful. The next day, with the help of my notes, I marked the route on my map sheets using a red pen. That was the first two days riding charted. I felt that I was making real progress, but would have to wait until I saw Laurie again in order to fill in the next two days.

A FRIEND FOR

DANNY-BOY

One day, early in February, I telephoned my old school friend Mary to arrange a day when I could drive over to see her. We had to work out a route from Bedale over to the A19. On the Thursday afternoon, during the week of my ride, we would be travelling from Bedale to Mary's farm, which lies between the river Swale and Kirby Wiske. Finding a route for this section proved to be the most difficult of the entire ride. The three main obstacles for horses were the A1, the Swale and the airfield at R.A.F. Leeming.

I arrived at Mary's around nine-thirty and after a quick drink of coffee we set off on our quest. Horses are not allowed on motorways and we would have to decide which of the three possible flyovers on the A1 would be the most suitable. There was only one place to cross the Swale and that was over a disused railway bridge. The river itself has high embankments and is extremely deep throughout this section, so impossible for the horses to ford. There was no way through without going close to the airfield. The jets on training days land and take-off every five minutes, making a horrendous noise, and possibly spooking the horses not used to such deafening sounds.

We spent most of the morning visiting friends with horses and farmers over whose land we might need to cross. Over lunch, Mary made several phone calls then we again checked out other routes. I felt that we hadn't really sorted anything but Mary was optimistic, as usual. She is not one to give in without a fight and promised to keep working on it.

The following week, I again went over to Mary's for a day. Since my last visit she had contacted more people. We started at her farm and followed the route passing Kirby Wiske. We crossed over the main north-south railway line and headed toward Thirsk. A couple of miles further on, Mary pointed out the bridleway that would take us to South Kilvington, then we drove round on the road to where the bridleway rejoined the road. I memorised the way through the village, under the A19 and on to the road heading for Felixkirk. This was as far west as Mary could help me, so we turned back and had a quick lunch.

Feeling refreshed, we set out to visit more farmers but without much luck. The first had gone on holiday and the next was out for the day. We journeyed on, travelling north to Bedale and back down the A1 to a farm lying on the west side of the Swale. This farmer *was* at home and most sympathetic to our predicament. He generously lent us his four-track vehicle to travel across the fields to see if there was any way through by the embankment. When we stopped to open a gate, a van pulled up behind us and the driver greeted Mary cheerfully. What luck! It was the local blacksmith. Mary introduced us and I asked him if I could contact him. He gave me his phone number saying he'd be happy to oblige us, should the need arise. We continued our search along the embankment but, as Mary had thought, every gate was padlocked. Sensing my disappointment, she told me not to worry, she would sort it out, but I was still feeling bad about it when I left for home. For the first time I wondered if, despite Mary's optimism, this might turn out to be a serious problem.

I tried to put these thoughts behind me, when later Allan and I discussed which would be the best week for the ride. We finally decided on the third week in May. Hopefully the weather would be reasonable by then but not too hot for the horses. I had first thought of riding in April, but Allan thought there might still be snow on the Pennines. He also realised that Maggie would still be busy helping with the lambing.

I couldn't go until late in May, as I would be performing with our local musical society. The show would be running in Whitby Theatre for five days, from the eighth to the thirteenth of May. I would also be busy rehearsing most nights during the previous week. Sunday the twentieth was the day we decided we would start our adventure. This would give me a week after the show closed to prepare for the ride. I marked a huge star in my diary.

Our little meetings were taking place around every three weeks, and I tried to forget about the worrying problems over the route for the Thursday afternoon. Carol kept bringing me large piles of letters to sign and post. Now that the dates were fixed, we could start on the posters that were to be displayed in the towns and villages along the route. I had to work out the approximate times of our arrival in each place. We were also trying to think of different ideas to attract publicity in order to draw the crowds and take maximum collections.

All the while the planning was going ahead, I was riding Danny-Boy to keep him fit and in late February I found him a companion. I was told about a five-year-old mare for sale and made arrangements to go and look at her. As soon as I saw her, I immediately took a fancy to her and after having a trial ride, was keen to buy her. We agreed on a fair price considering the horse's age and lack of experience. I knew that I wouldn't lose money on her, as I would increase her value after much work and training. Cloey was a chestnut thoroughbred with a white blaze down her face, and reminded me very much of my old mare, Ruby, which probably influenced my desire to buy her.

Cloey proved to be a delightful little horse. She was very gentle and kind natured, a real pleasure to have around, and Danny-Boy got on well with his new charge. Cloey had much to learn. But with guidance from me and example from Danny-Boy, she learnt quickly and daily became more confident. It gave me a certain peace of mind knowing that I had another horse to fall back on, should anything happen to Danny-Boy during the ride.

Then Mary rang to say that she was fairly sure that she'd finally managed to find a way through to her farm. Some of her riding friends were going to test it out at the weekend and were also going to ride with Maggie and myself from Bedale to show us the way. This was a great relief and I hoped and prayed it would be O.K.

TRAINING

INTENSIFIES

Sometimes Allan would ride out with me, when time allowed, but it was my daughter, Sara, who was delighted to have the opportunity to ride again. She is an accomplished rider but hadn't had the chance to ride much since her marriage. The youngest of her three children had just started school, leaving her with a little more free time.

She came over from Glaisdale once a week, and we usually rode about ten or twelve miles. I always looked forward to my rides with Sara, and we always went, no matter what the weather and had a lot of fun. As we were both very busy, our rides together gave us the opportunity to catch up on local gossip and family news and the riding helped take my mind off the constant planning.

Sometimes, I would ring Maggie and arrange to meet up with her and Cammy. We would talk excitedly about our week away together, and by now Maggie was determined to come. The horses loved these rides together, remembering each other from the days when Danny-Boy was just a youngster. It was different now though, Danny-Boy had matured and adopted a protective attitude towards Cammy. He had become the herd leader.

We continued to hold our meetings on a regular basis and Kathy managed to come to most of them. She was attending to the legal side of things - permits to take street collections had to be secured from every council through whose jurisdiction we would be riding, and insurance needed sorting out. One of my tasks was to obtain parking permission for the Land Rover and trailer in Bedale and Helmsley. I had to apply through the relevant police force and this was never straightforward. I was constantly being passed from one person to another and not always achieving much.

During one of our meetings, Laurie happened to drop in for a short visit on his way back home. He brought good news and bad. He had been unable to find us accommodation for our night in the Hawes area and had not found any suitable grazing. His good news was that he and Linda suggested we all stay two nights with them, transporting the horses from our finish on the Tuesday night back to their house. The next morning, we would take them back to where we'd stopped the previous day. This seemed feasible so I accepted his very kind offer.

I then took out my route maps and Laurie showed me, as near as possible, our route for the Wednesday. I marked this with my red pen, and Laurie was getting quite excited and said he hoped to ride with us from Hawes to Middleham. I was delighted to hear this, and I now had the route for the first three days on my maps.

I had worked out my route from Helmsley to Runswick Bay, where we would finish, and as this was all home territory it did not need checking. The only stretch left to chart, assuming Mary's new plan would work out, was from Felixkirk to Helmsley. Armed with maps and notepad, I set off with Allan one fine Sunday in March and headed for Felixkirk. From here we followed the narrow lanes through tiny villages until we found the bridleway up through the woods to the top of Sutton Bank. We returned to the Thirsk road and found where the same bridleway ended near Cold Kirby. A few miles further on, another bridleway branched off down a forest track through to Rievaulx Abbey. Again we travelled round to where this bridleway rejoined the road and I was able to fill in all this part of the route. It had all seemed simple compared with some of the other places.

Danny-Boy had never done much travelling in a horse-trailer, so we made plans to borrow a double trailer to take him and Cloey out together to give him some experience. Each Sunday for a few weeks, Allan and I loaded up the horses, travelled about an hour and took them for a two-hour ride. Cloey was used to being boxed and Danny-Boy soon walked in and out of the trailer without any fuss.

On one of these Sunday rides, we took the horses high on the moors above Farndale. Although the roads were clear, there was still snow in places and some of the tracks had filled in with drifting snow. I don't think Cloey had ever experienced such conditions before and was very apprehensive as she struggled to follow Danny-Boy through the deep drifts. He didn't mind at all, as I had ridden him out in all weathers. The air was cold and fresh and it felt as if we had the world to ourselves as we cantered along with the wind in our faces. The cold air made our eyes water and as we trotted back to our trailer I thought how lucky we were to share such wonderful rides together.

In April, while we still had the trailer, we bought tickets for a fund raising event organised by one of the local hunts. This was called a

'Pub Ride' and consisted of a huge breakfast at a local Inn followed by a twelve mile ride with stops at three more public houses. At each place (as well as drinks), there was a competition. Each contestant's score was totalled to find a winner at the end of the day.

Allan and I arrived in good time and, after breakfast, unloaded the horses and waited until our names were called. We set off at intervals, in groups of ten or more, each group having its own guide. We had to stick to the set course but could ride at whatever pace we liked. The terrain was varied and included moorland tracks, steep pathways and long flat grassy stretches where you could have a really good gallop.

The completed ride would bring us back to the starting point and as we were setting off, some of the earlier riders were returning, passing us on their homeward stretch. Cloey did very well and managed the difficult stretches better than I'd hoped. She enjoyed the gallops and didn't panic too much when we had to cross a wider and deeper river than she'd previously encountered.

Allan said that it was the best ride he'd had on Danny-Boy and everyone was in high spirits. We couldn't stay too long as we had to get the horses home but we'd had a wonderful day. Allan was now convinced that Danny-Boy was more than capable of carrying me across the North of England.

MY COMPANION

CONFIRMED

I didn't see much of Maggie during April as it was the lambing season, and the weather could not have been worse. She and Chris were kept very busy, but Maggie still tried to keep Cammy fit by using her to go round the sheep that they kept on another farm. Although most of their flock consisted of moor sheep and should have lambed outside, the land was so wet there was no dry lying. This meant that they had to bring them under cover until the lambs were a few days old and could tolerate the outside conditions. As each day passed and the weather didn't improve, finding space under shelter was becoming more difficult. They worked from dawn until long after dark in snow and rain, trying to save each newborn lamb. Many lambs were lost and some ewes didn't survive the awful conditions.

Maggie told me later it was like travelling through a long black tunnel that she thought would never end. Throughout the lambing she still had her family to feed and care for, and every night she went to bed exhausted, still hearing the pitiful bleating of lambs and their mothers in her ears. One thought kept her going through those long, cold, wet days and that was our 'Big Ride.'

Spring arrived at last bringing new hope and life. Daffodils were bravely pushing their heads through the cold damp earth and the lambs skipped and played in the watery sunshine. I spoke to Maggie on the phone and how great it was to hear again the happiness in her voice and her infectious laughter once more.

Early in May, she rode over to see me on Cammy. I greeted her with a huge hug, tears of joy in my eyes. We tied Cammy in the stable and went inside for a coffee. We chatted and laughed, making lists of things we would need to take with us. A vet had examined Cammy, and to Maggie's delight had said the horse was fit and healthy for her age, and quite capable of doing the ride.

Maggie had more good news. After the nightmare of the past month, she had persuaded Chris to take two days off and come to Bentham with us. I was so pleased as I knew it would be a welcome break for him. We chatted a while longer and then I saddled Danny-Boy up and rode halfway to Rosedale with Maggie. I waved her good-bye and, gathering up the reins, turned round and took a different track down the moor towards home. I let Danny-Boy have his head as we cantered along, feeling very happy. The world was a good place and I was so lucky. I prayed to God that we would all remain well and healthy, so that nothing would stop us going on our great adventure.

The planning was going along very nicely. I was receiving lots of replies from my letters, many of which enclosed donations. These ranged from five pounds up to a hundred pounds and were all banked into a special account that I had opened. I now had to find volunteers who would take the street collections in the towns and villages through which we would be travelling. I was able to persuade friends and relatives to take this on for the last two days of the ride. When I next spoke to Mary, she agreed to organize the collections on the

Thursday and Laurie had already told me that he would sort something out for the Wednesday. This left me with just the first two days over on the West side.

At our next meeting, we decided on the wording for the posters, which were to advertise our arrival at each stopping place. It had taken me quite a while but, using my maps to study the mileage, I had finally worked out the approximate times we would be riding through each venue. The posters bore the L.R.F. Logo and Ian agreed to type up the details. I reported on the response to our letters, detailing all amounts received so far. Carol and Ian were both delighted and we felt as if all our hard work was beginning to reap rewards.

Carol had more good news. She had talked her husband Joe into taking two days off work, so that they, too, could come to Bentham for the first two days of the ride. This was great and could also solve a problem for me. I asked Carol if she thought Joe would do the collecting for me on those two days. She said that she was sure he would be happy to and promised to ask him. I felt really good about all this and was beginning to feel that we had a really good team with a most enthusiastic spirit.

I gave Carol the number of the Inn where Maggie and Chris had booked their stay in Bentham and Carol rang later to say that she had talked her Dad into going too and had managed to secure accommodation for them all. This was wonderful. To have so much support and encouragement at the beginning of our ride could only be good. I rang Maggie with the news and she was equally thrilled, saying it would be like a big send-off party. I could sense the excitement in her voice. Only three more weeks and we'd be setting off.

A couple of days later, Ian left the completed posters in my porch. I sorted them into piles and posted several to Marie, Laurie and Mary. They had kindly agreed to display them in their areas. I would have to deliver the remainder by hand. I decided it was time I paid Dawne a visit so, armed with a sponsor sheet and the posters, I set off in my car over the moors to Helmsley.

It was a beautiful afternoon as I climbed out of the valley up on to the high moors. Bright green leafy areas of Bilberry plants contrasted sharply with the golden brown of the dead bracken patches, but in sheltered pockets on the bank sides I spotted small fronds of new bracken already emerging, waiting to unfurl. I decided to ride down through Farndale to see the wild daffodils.

What a glorious sight they made. Swathes of yellow in field after field by the edge of the stream making a spectacular scene. As I drove closer past them I could see hundreds of their golden trumpets nodding in the gentle breeze. No wonder people come in coach loads to see them.

I hadn't visited Dawne for quite some time so it was lovely to see her again. We settled down with a cup of coffee and caught up with all the family news. I told her all about the plans we'd made. We discussed the arrangements she'd made for the horses staying overnight in her fields. Dawne had just accepted an invitation to go on a last minute holiday with some friends which meant, unfortunately, that she would not be around when we rode into Helmsley but her daughter, Annabel, was more than willing to help. Dawne had four daughters who had all been in the local Pony Club and Annabel had continued riding and kept a show-jumper of her own. I knew our horses would be in capable hands.

Later, as we walked to the fields where Danny-Boy and Cammy would stay, Dawne had a surprise for me. She showed me the paddock where Annabel would corral the horses, then invited me to come down to the next field. I felt a lump in my throat as a familiar face came towards us. Her back was a little sunken betraying her eighteen years, but the same intelligent face and kind eye of Ruby hadn't aged at all. I swallowed hard and called her name. I'm sure she recognized my voice, but as of old, she only came to within a few feet of me. Dawne explained that the people who now owned Ruby didn't have grazing, so she was spending the summer here. It was wonderful to see her again and to know that she was being well cared for. As I walked back to my car I wondered if Ruby would recognize her son three weeks from now.

A HECTIC TWO

WEEKS

Tuesday of the following week was the opening night for our show 'Annie Get Your Gun'. I was in the chorus line singing and dancing, and after weeks working hard at rehearsals it was great to be performing in front of a live audience. The show ran for five nights, finishing on the Saturday. It was a huge success and I was sad but happy when it was over, as I could now concentrate on Danny-Boy.

The next morning I began increasing Danny-Boy's rations to build up his energy. After breakfast I saddled him up and headed for the moors. I loved my rides out alone with him and over the years we'd built up a wonderful relationship. He seemed to understand my moods and I knew this seven-day ride was asking a lot of a six year old but I felt he could do it and wouldn't let me down.

But could I do it? Doubts kept creeping into my mind. We would have to ride about twenty-five miles a day. I was used to riding long days in the saddle but not seven consecutive days. But I had to do it. There were so many people expecting it now, and so much money had been sponsored on me that I couldn't let them down. I occasionally spoke to Danny-Boy as we rode quietly along but otherwise there was little to disturb the tranquility around us. The early sunlight made the dew glisten on the intricate patterns of the spiders' webs. They seemed like shawls made of delicate gossamer threads, stretched across the heather stalks, like washing hung out to dry.

The curlews were calling and swooping overhead, warning their young of our presence. The golden plovers, too, were anxious as we drew near to them, for although I couldn't see them, I could hear their plaintive cries across the heather. The grouse were also busy guarding their nests and newly hatched chicks. Occasionally, the male bird would call out in alarm if he considered we were a danger to his family. I have to watch carefully as I ride the tracks at this time of year, always mindful of what damage a horse's hoof can do.

Danny-Boy listens to me as we ride along, one ear flicking back and forth. He understands my voice and I have complete trust in him. I know that if the success of the ride were down to him alone, we'd do it. As we hit the hard road, I was relieved to hear the regular clip-clop of metal on tarmac' - no shoes lost!

My farrier, David, had been earlier in the week to fit Danny-Boy with a new set of shoes. He wanted them to have a week to settle before I set off on my ride. He wouldn't take payment, saying that was his donation towards my venture and promised they would last the week! I thanked him and he wished me the best of luck.

Later in the day, my brother Tony and his wife came. They were going to stay in our house while we were away to look after our dogs and other animals, so needed to get to know their routines. It was good to see them and have a drink and chat together. Seven days later they would be back and we would be on our way.

The final week passed quickly as I had lots to do. May is always a very busy time in the garden as I try to complete all the planting out and now I was frantically working all hours to get as much done as was possible. Fortunately, the weather was favourable and I managed to plant all the Chrysanthemums and most of the Asters, leaving Stella with as little watering to do as possible.

Kathy came over, bringing the 'Finish' banner that was to be displayed at the hotel in Runswick Bay where our ride ended. She was also pleased to tell me that she had at last received the final permit for carrying out the street collections.

On the Wednesday, Mary rang to finally confirm that the route through to her farm was sorted, which was a huge relief.

On the Friday evening, Sara arrived as usual with the grandchildren. They came each week and stayed overnight. Jimmy, the eldest, was seven, Adam, a year younger and Josie was almost five. They were now getting very excited about their Nan's big ride. I had explained why I was doing it and how long it would take. Now that it was only two days away it had become more real to them. I got my usual hug from Josie and Adam approached me shyly with a small parcel in his hand. He said it was a present for Nan from all of them for doing this big ride. Smiling, I blinked back the tears and opened my present, which was a compact set of lipsticks. I told them that I would take it with me and that night, I was given extra big hugs and kisses when I tucked them up in bed. Nan going away was something they hadn't experienced before and the concern showed in their loving little faces.

Saturday was busy. After the children went home, I took Danny-Boy out for a short ride then set to with last minute jobs. There was washing, vacuuming, tack to clean and more items to add to my growing list. In the evening, Allan and I went to church, as was our normal practice. I prayed for a safe and successful journey and especially that the horses would remain free from injuries. After Mass, lots of friends approached me to say good-bye and wish me luck. It was good to know they would be thinking of me while I was away.

Later in the evening, Allan and I drove over to Rosedale for a drink at the local pub. I tried to relax and not worry about the next day. Our friend Mick was there and was asking if we were all prepared for our journey. He told us he was going to try and ride part of the way with me on the Saturday and Sunday. It would depend on how poorly he was feeling, as he was due in hospital on the Friday for more chemotherapy. The courage and determination that had inspired me to raise money for Leukaemia Research never ceased to amaze me. I hoped he would be able to ride some of the way, as I knew how much it would mean to him. Travelling home, I was filled with mixed emotions. Anxiety, anticipation, excitement, and doubts in my own ability were all racing round my mind. I would go home and try to sleep. Tomorrow was almost here.

OUR JOURNEY BEGINS

I awoke with a feeling of anticipation and excitement. At last, the day I had long been waiting for had arrived. All the planning that had taken six months to do was now finished. Today I would be setting off on my 'Big Ride'. I lay awhile thinking about the week ahead. Doubts again flitted through my mind. What had I let myself in for? Could I really ride all those miles? Would Danny-Boy stay sound the whole week? Hundreds of pounds had been promised by sponsors and I shivered as the fear of letting them down gripped me. This was silly, I told myself. I jumped out of bed, thinking of all the things I had to do and pushed all thoughts of failure from my mind.

After breakfast, Allan and I exercised all the dogs, just a little sad that we wouldn't be seeing them for nearly a week. During coffee, we went over my check-list adding last minute items that we thought we might need. Next, we drove to Lealholm with the Land Rover to pick up the trailer from our friends, Nick and Charlotte. When we arrived back home, we set about trying to fix the huge red L.R.F. banners to either side of the trailer. While we were still struggling with the banners, Stella, Tony's wife, arrived. It was good to see her, and, helpful as always, she set to in the kitchen where the breakfast pots were still sitting in the sink. Gratefully, I left her to it and continued helping Allan. When at last the banners were secure, I went inside to start the packing.

First, I started with everything I would need for Danny-Boy, for after all, he was the most important one. Spare numnahs, reins, towels, rubbers, grooming kit and his first aid box, which I hoped we wouldn't need, were all packed into the first case. I later added other items of tack and my saddlebag. My spare saddle would go straight into the Land Rover. Next, I packed a case for Allan and myself. I also had a list of items connected with the L.R.F. This included collecting boxes, identity badges, permits, tabards and forms for the collectors to sign. I was terrified that I would forget something.

Allan, in the meantime, was loading up the trailer, leaving one side free for Danny-Boy. Allan's list included barrels of water, bags of horse feed, feeding bowls, water buckets, hay-nets, horse sheets and a brush and shovel for emergency clean-ups. Bags of haylage were hoisted on to the roof rack just in case the grazing wasn't sufficient.

I was supposed to be cooking lunch but Stella had taken over, so I

continued helping Allan with the rest of the packing. Suitcases, saddles, wellies, riding boots, hat, crop, waterproofs and coats all had to be squashed into the back of the Land Rover. Again, I referred to my checklist and carried into the Land Rover camcorder, camera, field glasses, flasks and torch. Items for my saddlebag included string, mobile phone (lent to me by my son), penknife, first-aid kit and, most important, my little book of phone numbers.

Just before lunch, I went out to the field and called in the horses. As usual, Danny-Boy came running, followed closely by Cloey. She follows him everywhere and was really going to miss him after we'd gone. I tied them both in the stable and gave Danny-Boy a good feed of concentrates, giving Cloey just a handful to keep her happy. I had told Danny-Boy many times about our adventure and I'm sure he could sense the excitement in me. My mind was racing ahead as I stroked and groomed him ready for the journey. I couldn't wait for tomorrow.

After lunch, Allan and I washed and changed ready to go. I went over my list yet again, hoping we hadn't forgotten anything. Allan let down the tailgate while I brought Danny-Boy from the stable and walked him on to the grass to stale. He is well trained and it was going to be a long journey. He walked straight into the trailer but shouted to Cloey, wondering why she wasn't coming too. While Allan fastened the tailgate, I went back to the stable to say goodbye to Cloey and to turn her loose in the field.

At last, the time had come to bid our farewells. My close friend Joy had arrived as we were loading up Danny-Boy. She hugged me as she said goodbye, telling me everything would be fine. We had been good friends for many years and had much in common. Joy had a horse and we sometimes rode out together. She was also a member of our choir and we had been in the musical show together. I was glad she came. Our son Dave was there and Stella too, all waving us goodbye.

This was it then, I thought. There was no turning back now, we were on our way. I couldn't believe that we were really on the road after all the weeks and months of planning and preparing for this day.

I gazed at the familiar hills and fields around us as we pulled away from the house. I had a lot of miles to ride before I would see them again. Please, please let everything go all right, was my silent prayer.

It was a pleasant day with the sun occasionally breaking through the thin clouds as we drove over the moors, through familiar villages and on across country towards Leyburn. Mile after mile we drove and all the time I kept thinking to myself that I would have to ride all this way back. It seemed a daunting prospect. As we wound our way up Wensleydale and over the Pennines, there was mist and a little dampness in the air. Later, as we travelled down towards Ribblehead, the weather brightened and I gazed longingly up at the distant fells.

We pulled off the road and parked at the place where the track that we would be taking on Tuesday, left the road. It went through a gateway, over some rough pasture and across a shallow moorland stream, before climbing up the fell side. The views from up there must be wonderful. I checked on Danny-Boy to make sure he was okay, and then we had a drink of coffee before continuing on our way. We travelled through Ingleton and on to where our hosts for the next two nights lived, near Bentham.

We arrived about four-thirty and David and Marie were outside to greet us. We pulled off the road into the small paddock and unboxed Danny-Boy, who was none the worse for his long ride in the trailer. I led him down into the bottom field where he was soon grazing contentedly.

We took our luggage inside and unpacked before joining David and Marie for a cup of tea. They asked all about the planned ride, curious to know how everything had worked out. Later, we wandered outside, as it was such a lovely afternoon. I was just admiring their garden when a car pulled up by the house bearing Joe, Carol, and her father, Alf. I was amazed to see them, as I hadn't told them where we were staying. Joe's explanation was that he had just followed his nose.

I introduced them all to each other and the new arrivals were invited in for a drink. We sat around chatting and discussing the week ahead. There was an eager air of expectancy, like Christmas Eve when we were children. After a while, Joe said it was time they were going to find their accommodation. We waved them off, saying we would see them later in the evening. Now we had to wait for Chris and Maggie. I had given Maggie instructions on how to find us and they were hoping to arrive by five-thirty.

We were starting to get a little worried when there was a call on my mobile. It was Chris saying they were lost! As they didn't know the area at all, it was difficult for them to describe where they were so Allan and I set off in the Land Rover to look for them. After a couple more calls, we found them just outside Bentham. Very relieved, we led the way back to our new friends' home. Cammy had also travelled well, and was happy to join Danny-Boy in the paddock. Having given me instructions about Cammy's food for the morning, Maggie left with Chris to join the others at the hotel.

It was a beautiful evening, when later Allan and I drove through Bentham to join all our friends for an evening meal. It was a very special evening in that friendly bar where we all sat and ate and had a few drinks. There was an air of anticipation and excitement as we all laughed and talked together. Later in the evening my cousin Pete joined us, his company adding to that wonderful occasion. Maggie looked radiant and was eagerly looking forward to our week together. Chris smiled at everyone, looking like a little boy playing truant. He probably couldn't remember the last time he'd been away from the farm. I can't describe my feelings on that night, but I know the memory of it will stay with me forever.

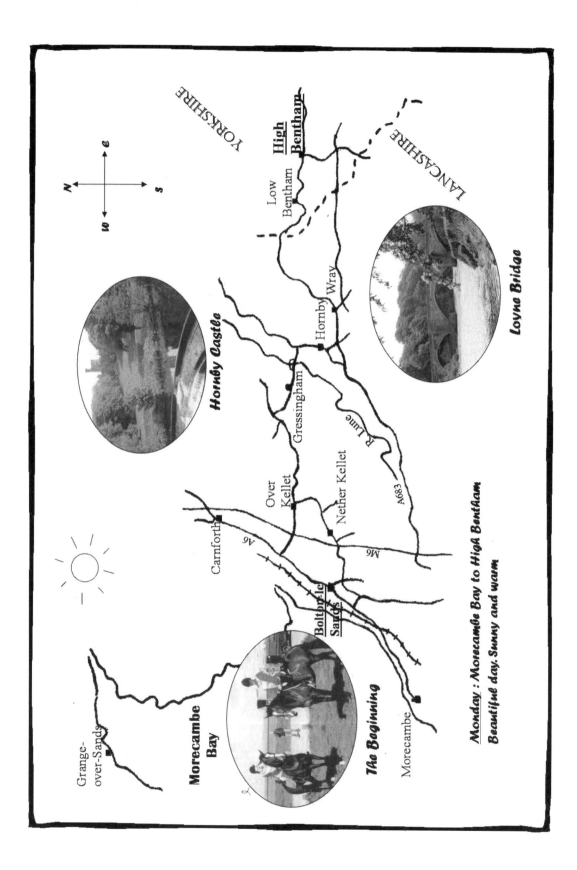

YORKSHIRE

LANCASHIRE

High Bentham

Low Bentham

Loyne Bridge

Hornby

Wray

Hornby Castle

Gressingham

R Lune

Over Kellet

Nether Kellet

A683

Carnforth

A6

M6

Boltbrle Sands

Morecambe Bay

Grange-over-Sands

The Beginning

Morecambe

Monday : Morecambe Bay to High Bentham
Beautiful day. Sunny and warm

Part II

MONDAY MAY 22

MORECAMBE BAY

TO

HIGH BENTHAM

"Allan,"

"Mm?"

"Allan, wake up, today's the day." I jumped out of bed and rushed to the window. My skin tingled with excitement.

"It's a lovely day Al, I can see all the fell tops as clear as a bell." I turned back to the room. Allan was sitting up in bed.

"I'd better be up then," he smiled at me. He is never one to show any great emotion but I knew underneath that he was almost as excited as I was. I dressed quickly, pulling on my jodhpurs, shirt and sweater. This would be my mode of dress for the next seven days. I rushed downstairs where I was greeted madly by Sheba, the Alsatian dog.

"Morning David," I announced cheerfully as I entered the kitchen. He looked up and smiled.

"Hi, did you sleep okay?"

"Yes, fine thanks," I replied.

"I'm just making a pot of tea, would you like a cup?"

"No thanks, not just yet, I'm going to feed the horses first, then I'll have my breakfast. Is Marie not up yet?"

"Oh yes, she's just popped down to Bentham to pick up Louise, she'll be back soon." I turned as I reached the door.

"I hope your daughter wasn't too put out at having to give up her room for us."

"Not at all," he replied. "She often stays with a friend on a weekend."

"Still, it was very good of her." I smiled and went outside. Early morning sunshine was filtering through broken clouds. I collected my lead-rope and walked down to the paddock where the horses were, admiring the amazing view as I went. I could see far across the moors towards Settle and over hills and farms to the South.

"Danny-Boy," I called out as I opened the gate. His head lifted when he heard my voice and he came trotting up the field. I clipped the lead-rope on him and walked him through the gateway. There was no need to lead Cammy because she was already following on behind Danny-Boy. They both looked fine with no sign of any stiffness after their long journey in the trailers.

As I walked back up the field, I saw Al coming out of the house and called to him as he walked over to the trailer.

"It's a great day, aren't we lucky?" He came to meet me with a lead-rope in his hand.

"Aye, if it stays like this all week you'll do well," he replied, taking hold of Cammy's head-collar and clipping on her lead-rope.

"Better not put them too close together," I said, as we hitched them to the fence. "We don't want any accidents before we've even started. Can you fetch Cammy's food, please? Maggie put it all ready in a bowl in the trailer and I'll get Danny-Boy's." Soon, both horses were munching avidly and we left them to go and have our own breakfast. We were just sitting down at the table when Marie came back.

"Hello everyone, it's a beautiful morning, isn't it? I noticed the horses chomping away out there. I expect you're dying to get started, Ann," she said.

"Yes, I can't wait," I replied excitedly. "I thought today would never come." We all chatted away through breakfast, then I paid a last visit to the bathroom before going out to find my riding boots and start grooming Danny-Boy. Al soon followed and was just putting the feed bowls away when Chris and Maggie arrived. Maggie was beaming.

"Hi everyone, hope we aren't late. Are the horses okay, did

Cammy eat all her food up?" she asked, all in one breath.

"No, you're not late and yes, to the other questions," I replied laughing. "Isn't it a great morning?" Chris was walking towards us, having just parked their vehicle.

"Couldn't wish for better weather when yer on 'oliday," he grinned at me.

"I'm *not* on holiday," I replied, smiling back at him. Chris was always teasing me about never going on holiday.

"Life's one long holiday for Ann," Allan quipped, winking at Chris. I ignored that comment and concentrated on getting Danny-Boy saddled and bridled. Soon we had the horses all loaded up and we were ready to start our trip over to the coast. David and Marie came out to see us leave. I called to them through the window of the Land Rover.

"Don't forget we're taking you out tonight, so don't start cooking dinner!" I waved goodbye and we were off down the road with Chris and Maggie following on behind us. I tried to concentrate on the map, as we'd only been on this road once before but I could hardly sit still, I was so excited. We passed through Bentham and on to the roadside pub by the river, where Carol and Joe, with Alf, joined the convoy and we all continued our journey to Morecambe Bay.

We found the narrow lane that turned off the main road from Bolton-le-Sands and made our way down towards the sea front. I climbed down from the Land Rover and I could hear the sea in the distance. Sea-gulls were calling and circling overhead. Over to the right, beyond the grassy mudflats and sandbeds, I could see right across to Grange-over-Sands. The tide was low and right down near the shoreline, I could just make out someone walking a dog.

I noticed another vehicle already parked on the hard standing as I closed the Land Rover door. A gentleman got out of the vehicle and started walking towards us. I went to meet him.

"Good morning, are you Ann Bowes, the lady doing the coast-to-coast ride?" he enquired. He smiled at me curiously.

"Yes, I am," I replied. He held out his hand.

"I'm Robert Jackson, a freelance reporter and I wondered if you could give me a few more details about your ride? I'd like to give you a write-up in our local *Gazette*." I shook his outstretched hand warmly.

"Certainly, I'd be glad to." Our little interview took about five minutes and he promised to send me a cutting of his piece from the paper. In return, I promised to send him all the details of the completed ride and let him know the final amount of money raised. He thought it would be good to do a follow-up article. He again took my hand.

"Thank you very much and good luck on your ride." He walked back to his car. As I turned to see how Allan was doing with Danny-Boy, I recognised a cheery familiar face approaching me.

"Kathy, how great to see you."

"I had to come and see you setting off. After being involved in all the planning, I wanted to make sure you got away all right," she joked. "I'm on holiday in Kirby Lonsdale with a friend for the week, so it wasn't too far to pop down this morning."

"Well, it's very good of you. I hope the weather stays like this all week, for both of us," I added with a grin, as we walked over to the horses.

"Yes, it would be nice. Good luck anyway and I'll see you back at Runswick." She pulled something from her pocket. "This is for Danny-Boy," she said, stroking him. I took the bright red sash, showing the L.R.F. logo that she handed me.

"Thanks Kathy, I'm sure he'll be very proud to wear it." I took her over to Maggie and introduced them to each other before going back to the Land Rover to find the tabards we had to wear. These, too, were bright red like the sash and we would be wearing them all the time that we were riding. I called to Maggie, who was busy adjusting Cammy's girth. She asked Chris to hold Cammy and came over to me. I held out one of the tabards for her.

"They'll certainly see us coming in these, won't they?" she said. She put it over her head and was laughing as she added, "might just about cover my bum."

"There's nowt wrong with your bum," Allan was grinning at her as he led Danny-Boy over towards us. "Mind, there might be before't week's out."

"Well, it's certainly well padded and so is my saddle, so I'm sure I'll be fine," Maggie laughed back at him.

While they were chatting, I went and found my saddlebag and Allan helped me fix it to the saddle. More people were arriving, including some on horseback from the local riding club. One of these offered to ride a short distance with us and see us through the town. It was almost time for us to leave, so I went to find my riding hat and was looking for my crop in the back of the Land Rover, when a voice spoke behind me.

"I'm just in time then?" I turned round in surprise, beaming,

"Pete! Oh, I'm so glad you were able to come, how did you manage it?"

"With difficulty," he grinned. "I sneaked out of work for an hour." He gave me a big hug. "Had to come and wish you luck, didn't I? I'm hoping I might get to join you tonight, too."

"Oh, I hope so, that would be great." I squeezed his hand. It meant a lot to me, seeing him this morning. He must have felt my apprehension.

"Not nervous are you?" he quizzed. "You'll do great, you always do."

"Thanks Pete, I hope you're right."

"I must be going now, they'll start missing me at work." He smiled, jumped back in his car and was gone.

By now, Joe had put on his tabard and was busy taking the collecting box round. He was going to travel with Allan in the Land Rover while Carol took her Dad on a tour round the countryside. Alf had been stationed in this area during the war, so this would be a trip down memory lane for him. At last, Maggie and I were both mounted up and ready to go. Allan and Chris were busy video recording and Kathy and Carol were snapping away with their cameras. Danny-Boy was full of himself, pawing at the ground and tossing his head impatiently. Then we were off! To shouts of 'Goodbye,' 'Don't fall off,' 'Good luck' and 'See you later' ringing in our ears, we set off up the little lane at a brisk trot.

At last, my ride had begun. For months, I had worked and planned for this day. Now all I had to do was ride! Every care and precaution had been taken and now it was up to Danny-Boy and myself. I knew that my faith in him was not unfounded.

We soon reached the end of the little lane leading to the busy Morecambe road and turned left. After a hundred yards, we reached the main road, which we had to cross, and, led by our friendly guide, took a quiet back way through Bolton-le-Sands. Once clear of the town, Danny-Boy led the way and our friend chatted all the time as she tried to keep up with him.

"How old is your horse?"

"He's six," I replied.

"How long did you have to train him for this ride?"

"Well, I didn't have to train him, but I had to get him very fit and that took about six months."

"How long will it take you to reach the east coast? Will you have to have rest days?"

"No, we're expecting to complete it in seven days," I replied

"I think it's a lot of riding. Won't you get saddle-sore?" she asked. I smiled.

"No, I don't think so. I'm used to spending long days in the saddle." She continued her chatter for another mile, then said that she would have to leave us. I thanked her very much for coming along and giving us her support. She turned, waved goodbye and trotted off back down the road. Maggie trotted up along side me, grinning.

"Phew, that's a relief."

"Yes, I was thinking the same thing. She was a sweet lady but I'm glad she wasn't riding all day with us."

"Do you think she *ever* stops talking?" asked Maggie.

"I don't know," I answered. "Maybe she thought we'd expect her to chatter all the time." We trotted on in amicable silence until we heard the roar of heavy traffic.

"That must be the motorway ahead," I commented. "I wonder how the horses will react." Neither of the horses had ever been near a motorway.

"Don't know," Maggie replied, "but we'll soon find out." As we approached the flyover, Danny-Boy's head went up, ears pricked, listening to the roar. Maggie went first with Cammy, as usually nothing worries her and she trotted over, unconcerned. I urged Danny-Boy to follow. He wasn't sure which side of the road he wanted to be on. First edging one way, then the other, as traffic roared both ways beneath us, he cautiously made his way across the flyover.

"It's okay, old fella, just keep walking," I said, as I urged him forward. Much to his relief, we were soon on the other side, catching up with Cammy.

"Was he okay?" Maggie shouted back to me.

"Well, not too bad," I answered, as I came along side her. "Cammy did well, didn't she?"

"Yes, I was quite surprised. We don't see that much traffic up Rosedale," she laughed. We trotted on through Nether Kellet and on to Over Kellet, where Allan was waiting at the crossroads to see how we'd managed over the motorway. After a quick word, we continued our journey. Apart from a few miles on the busy Kirby Lonsdale to Carnforth road, traffic was fairly quiet.

We were riding through some beautiful countryside. The land was undulating, with small fields and old-fashioned hedgerows. Scattered here and there were little copses and woods. It had a sleepy air about it, making me think that this was what most of rural England must have looked like many years ago. The sun was high in the sky, making it feel quite warm and it was tiring for the horses, mile after mile on the hard road. Eventually, we rode down into the quiet village of Gressingham.   Trees lined the road and stone built-houses overlooked the neat, well-tended gardens. We never saw a soul as we trotted on towards the river Lune. It was really quite hot now and Maggie had removed her sweater, tying it round her waist.

As we approached the Loyn Bridge, a wonderful stone structure, I paused to watch some birds darting about above the water.

"Maggie, look, what do you think those birds are?"

"I'm not sure. They look a bit like swallows, don't they? Except they're more brownie coloured."

"They're going in and out of those holes in the riverbank. I think they must be sandmartins," I said. "I know they nest in vertical bank sides but I thought they kept more to the cliffs." We watched them a while longer, swooping and diving across the water and then back over the field above the bank.

"I must ask Al, he'll know what they are." We turned to cross the bridge.

"I hope we don't meet anything." Maggie looked a little apprehensive. The bridge could only carry single file traffic. There were triangular shaped alcoves at intervals, where a cyclist or pedestrian could get out of the way of a vehicle but they weren't suitable for a horse. We trotted briskly over, thankful to reach the other side without meeting anything.

Ten minutes later, we arrived in Hornby and soon found the Royal Oak, our rendezvous for lunch. All the others were already there and Allan was filling the water buckets for the horses.

"I bet they're ready for this," he said. "It's turned out hot, hasn't it?" I slid down from the saddle, ran the irons up and loosened the girth.

"Yeah, I think we'll all appreciate a drink. I'll get his food out, Al." Maggie had taken Cammy's saddle off to let her back cool down. Cammy tended to sweat up more as her saddle had a thicker numnah on and an extra cover on the saddle. Maggie felt it put less pressure on Cammy's back. She was, after all, getting on a bit.

"Chris and I will hold the horses while you and Maggie go inside and get your lunch." Allan came and took the reins from me.

"Thanks, I'm certainly ready for a drink. Come on Maggie, let's go inside." Carol and her Dad were already seated at a table and Joe followed us in, bringing his collecting box.

"Might as well try our luck in here," he said, smiling.

Jim Bowen, famed for 'Bull's Eye' on television, had once owned the Inn. He had redecorated it in a maritime theme. It was nice and cool inside and several customers were already eating. We ordered our drinks and sandwiches and took a welcome seat at the bar. When Alf and Carol finished their lunch, they went to tend the horses so that Allan and Chris could have theirs.

The landlord asked Maggie and me about our ride and put a generous donation in Joe's box. He then said it was fine for Joe to approach his customers, all of whom gave a contribution. Our half-hour break passed quickly and it was time to get ready once more. The horses had enjoyed their drink, a small ration of hand food and had also been allowed a short nibble of grass.

Having tightened my girth, I jumped back into the saddle once more and waited for Maggie. She was soon ready and we set off walking down through the village. As we were crossing the bridge over the river, I stopped to exclaim.

"Maggie, look, isn't that lovely?"

"Ooh, yes, I must take a picture." She hunted in her pockets for her camera. Standing well back from the village, on a hill, was a beautiful old castle, framed by tall trees in all their verdant glory. Sloping down to the river from the castle, well-kept pastures, with sheep grazing contentedly, completed this picturesque scene.

"It's such a perfect picture, almost like a painting," I said. 'England in all her glory,' was the thought that came to mind. "Well, we'd best get going." I turned Danny-Boy down the road.

Once through the village, we put the horses into a trot and headed on towards Wray. We had to be on the lookout for traffic all the time, as the roads were narrow and full of bends. There were few, if any, grass verges and so it was again tiring for the horses, constantly travelling on the hard road. Having ridden about two miles, we arrived in Wray, a quaint, sprawling village with roads leading in all directions. From here, we took the quiet back road to Bentham, where we would eventually meet up with Allan and Joe again.

A few miles further on and we were back in Yorkshire. We still had many miles to go but that telling boundary sign gave me a lovely feeling of belonging and I felt just that much nearer to home. The road was very narrow but there was little traffic to bother us. We met the occasional farm tractor, a milk tanker and now and then a car. We were able to enjoy the peaceful, rural surroundings as we sometimes walked but mostly trotted the eight or nine miles back to Bentham. It was very warm and I was glad of my small bottle of juice in my saddlebag. Maggie, too, was grateful for one of the orange cartons that she always carried in her pocket.

We passed a few herds of cows that were contentedly chewing their cud in the afternoon sun. Sheep grazed quietly, their lambs frolicking and jumping about without a care in the world. We could smell the distinctive scent of the May blossom in full bloom in the hedgerows. As we passed by one particular garden, the wonderful smell of lilac drifted our way. There were many trees, especially oak and ash, growing among the hedges. Occasionally, in the fields, too, we saw them standing in solitary splendour, no doubt providing welcome shade from the hot mid-day sun for the livestock. Birds were singing and whistling in all the hedgerows. They'd be kept busy, I'm sure, finding food for their hungry young families. Now and then a cock-pheasant would call out and pigeons were heard cooing over in a nearby wood. It was hard to believe that another kind of world existed; we were so lost in our own.

We had been riding a couple of hours, when a car coming towards us, began to slow down.

"That's Carol's car, isn't it?" queried Maggie.

"Yes, you're right," I replied. As the car stopped, Carol wound her window down.

"How're you doing?" she asked, smiling up at us. "It's not much further, you'll be able to see Bentham, when you reach that next hill."

"Good," I answered, "we should make it on time then. Have you had a good day?"

"Yes, we've been all over, haven't we Dad?" she said, turning to Alf.

"Aye, it took mi back a few years but nut many spots 'ave changed much," he replied in his dry Yorkshire brogue.

"You'll be wanting to come back again, Alf," Maggie suggested.

"Aye, I might at that, if I 'ave some body ti drive me about," he grinned shyly at us.

"Well, we'd best let you get on or you won't be there on schedule," said Carol.

"See you both later then," I called as they pulled away. "It'll do Alf good, this little break."

"Yes," agreed Maggie. "It can't be that long since Carol's Mum died. He must miss her terribly." We rode on, deep in our thoughts.

Carol was right. As we rode over the brow of the next hill, there lay Bentham. Five minutes later, we were trotting towards the town and spotted the familiar red banners on the Land Rover. Joe jumped out as we approached.

"I'll walk alongside you in the High Street," he said. "It should be quite busy at this time of day." As we crossed the main street, which was bustling with people, a lady came running from the pub opposite.

"We thought we'd missed you," she uttered breathlessly. "I've been watching out for you all afternoon. Wait here a moment, please." With that, she dashed back inside the pub and a moment later reappeared, holding out a plastic bag, heavy with money.

"I read about you on a poster and took a collection round the bar but couldn't remember what time you were arriving."

"Thank you so much," I said, accepting the money. "People are very generous, aren't they?"

"Well, it's a good cause and I think you're both doing a great job. How far have you come today?" she asked.

Maggie answered her. "We've ridden from Morecambe Bay but we haven't much farther to go today."

"Gosh, that's a long way, you must be tired. I hope you do really well. Good luck!"

"Thanks," we both replied in unison. We bade her farewell and soon caught up with Joe down the High Street. He was doing a great job with the collecting box and grinned as I handed him the money.

"That'll give mi total a fair boost," he said. "We haven't done too bad for't first day." We eventually left the throngs of people and rode on through the residential area on the edge of the town. Allan was waiting ahead and Joe was just about to rejoin him when we heard voices and laughter.

"What's going on over there?" Maggie queried.

"I don't know," I replied. "Let's go and see." When there was a break in the traffic, we trotted over the road to look over a large hedge from where the noise was coming. We saw before us a beautiful manicured bowling green in front of a very smart pavilion. Several elderly ladies and gentlemen were enjoying a game in the afternoon sunshine. Surprised to see two horses and riders peering over the hedge at them, they wandered over to ask what the tabards were displaying. By this time, Joe had walked through the gate and down the steps to join the contestants. He explained to them what we were doing and why. They started talking to each other to find out who had any money.

"I never bring any money with me, only my bowling money," said one old lady.

"Have you got any, Norma?" she asked, turning to her friend.

"Not much," her friend replied, "but they can have all I can find." They searched their pockets and some returned to the pavilion hoping to find something for us.

"Thank you all very much, it's very kind of you," said Joe, as they each dropped their coins in his box. "I hope we didn't spoil your game."

"Not at all," answered one elderly gentleman. "We're glad you stopped by. We've got all evening to play." We waved goodbye to a sea of smiling faces and trotted off down the road.

"Just one mile to go," I said. "We're going to be back by half past four."

"We could go for a drive out, couldn't we?" Maggie asked. "It's too nice a day to stay indoors."

"Yeah, why not? We could go to Settle, I've never been there," I replied.

"Good idea," said Maggie, "I'm sure Chris and Allan will agree. We'll ask them anyway." As we trotted on making our plans, I gazed across to our left, beyond Ingleton.

"That's where we'll be riding tomorrow, Maggie." Her eyes followed my gaze.

"Up that valley to the left?"

"Yes," I replied, "beneath that long grey-looking rock face."

"Won't it be marvellous to get off the hard roads and away from the traffic? And then do we go up on to the Pennines?" she asked.

"Yes, after lunch. I can't wait to see the views from up there. It will be brilliant if it's like this." We walked the horses the last two hundred yards, letting them cool off. We explained to Chris and Al the plans we had made while we untacked the horses. The horses were given a drink and some hand food before we took them down to the paddock. As usual, Maggie had put the out-door sheet on Cammy.

"Are you sure she'll need that tonight?" I asked. "It's such a lovely warm evening."

"Yes, I know," replied Maggie, "but it may turn cooler later and she's used to having it on. Besides, the extra warmth helps to prevent her arthritis setting in." I'd no sooner shut the gate, than Danny-Boy was down on his back, legs in the air, enjoying a very energetic roll, first one way then the other. He stood up, kicked his back legs in the air and squealed out in delight, as if to say, "I sure needed that!"

"Well, that's the first day completed safe and sound, Maggie." We were walking back to the house. Chris was already waiting, with the engine running.

"Yeah, it went okay really but I'm ready for a nice long bath! We'll pick you up around five-thirty then, eh?" she asked, climbing into their vehicle.

"Yeah, great," I replied, as they pulled out of the yard.

Later, bathed and dressed in my jeans and tee shirt, I felt happy and refreshed as we all drove over to Settle. The sun was still shining and the stark tops of Ingleborough on our left, stood out against the clear blue sky. On our right, we could see far across to the distant moors. We laughed and talked as we drove along, enjoying the wonderful views and perfect weather. In Settle, we went our separate ways, arranging to meet up later. Maggie wanted to buy presents for Chris to take home to the children the next day. Allan and I strolled around the town square that was still quite busy. Eventually, we all met up and sat and ate an ice cream , outside the old town hall.

"You must be on 'oliday now, Ann?" Chris asked, pretending to be serious.

"Well, I must admit, I do feel a bit like a tourist," I laughed. We finished our ice cream and wandered back to the car park.

"Come on, I've bought a bottle of sherry. Let's have a drink to celebrate the success of our first day," I told them, as we climbed into the vehicle. I poured each of us a small measure into some paper cups.

"Cheers, everyone," said Maggie. "Here's to the rest of the week."

"Aye," said Al, "it's a shame you couldn't stay a bit longer, Chris."

"Oh, I don't know," grinned Maggie. "He might get a liking for t!" Soon we were back and waving them off once more, having arranged a time to meet up later. We joined David and Marie in their garden, enjoying the evening sunshine and told them all about the day's events. Time passed quickly and soon it was time to change for our evening out.

We all had a wonderful time together and all too soon, it was time to leave and make our way back home. On arriving, I walked down to peek at the horses while Marie popped Sheba out for a last walk. Cammy was lying down and Danny-Boy, with head hung low, was standing over her. I knew they were both sleeping. I smiled to myself, contentedly. Tomorrow was another day. I caught up with Marie and we returned to the house together.

"Thank you both very much for this evening," David said, looking at Allan and myself as we headed for the stairs.

"It was our pleasure," said Allan. "We've all had a great evening." He wished them both goodnight and went off to bed. I lingered a moment, wondering how to say what I wanted to tell them.

"I hate goodbyes, so I probably won't say a lot in the morning. I want you to know how much I appreciate what you've done for us. No, let me finish," as David started to speak. "It isn't every one who would take in two complete strangers as you have done and make them so welcome. Thank you both very much."

"I'm glad we were able to help," said Marie.

"I hope you'll let us know how the rest of the week goes," said David. "I'm sure you'll make lots of money. Please write to us when you find the time."

"I will," I promised, smiling. "Goodnight and God bless."

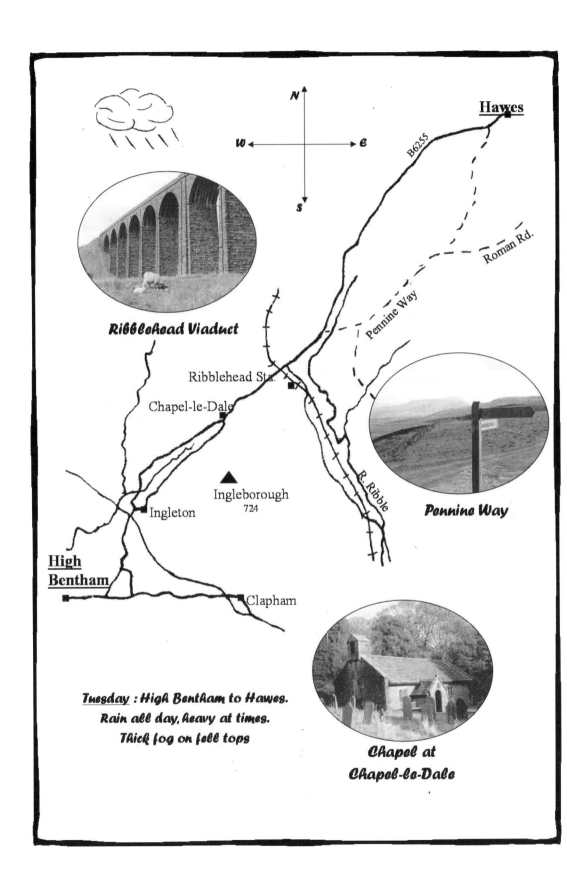

Hawes

N
W ← → E
S

B6255

Roman Rd.

Pennine Way

Ribblehead Viaduct

Ribblehead Sta.

Chapel-le-Dale

▲ Ingleborough
724

Ingleton

Pennine Way

R. Ribble

High Bentham

Clapham

Tuesday : High Bentham to Hawes.
Rain all day, heavy at times.
Thick fog on fell tops

Chapel at
Chapel-le-Dale

TUESDAY MAY 23

HIGH BENTHAM

TO HAWES.

I awoke with a feeling of dismay. I could hear the wind in the trees and the rain rattling against the window-panes. I rushed to the window, not wanting to believe what I saw. A gusty wind was blowing the branches of the trees all ways in the rain. I could barely make out the outline of houses in Ingleton, and the fell tops of Ingleborough were completely lost in dense fog. Realisation hit me.

"Allan, it's raining and blowing and Danny-Boy will be wet through," I cried. I dressed hurriedly as I continued, "How am I going to get him dry?"

"Stop panicking," Allan replied, "we've loads of time and I'll come and help you towel him down." He knew I couldn't put a saddle on his wet back. It could make him sore and I certainly didn't want that. I rushed downstairs and found David already there.

"What a morning, isn't it?" he greeted me woefully.

"Awful," I agreed. "Do you think I could borrow a coat and some wellies, please? All mine are in the Land Rover. I never expected this."

"Of course, take any that fit you," he answered. I found a Parka that was a bit too large and pulled the hood over my head. I put on some wellies that seemed to fit and off I went to get the lead rope and fetch the horses. They were both standing under the tree at the bottom of the paddock. Danny-Boy didn't need calling twice and I soon had them up by the fence. Allan was finding his coat from the Land Rover.

"What a morning. Where have you got the towels?" he asked.

"I'll find them if you can get their food," I replied. I found them underneath all the tack in Danny-Boy's case and quickly returned with them. Allan was putting the bowls of food down for the horses. Taking a towel each, we worked either side of Danny-Boy, rubbing his back vigorously.

"Go get another dry towel and we'll lay it folded on his saddle-patch. If we put his sheet over the top, it should dry out with his body heat," Allan suggested. I had to hold the towel in place as the wind kept whipping it away, while Al threw the sheet over. Soon we had the sheet securely in place and both horses were happily eating away at their food. We hurried back indoors, ready for a hot cup of tea. Marie was setting places at the table.

"This is a surprise. Who would have thought it would be like this after yesterday?" she said, adding, "I hope you've plenty of waterproofs."

"Yes, I have," I replied sitting down at the table. Over breakfast, I explained to her and David where we would be riding that day. They hoped that the weather would improve, but the forecast wasn't that great. After breakfast, Allan and I went upstairs to pack. As we were taking our cases to the Land Rover, Chris and Maggie arrived.

"You knew what you were doing last night, didn't you?" I said jokingly.

"What *do* you mean?" she asked innocently, a cheeky grin on her face.

"You will have a nice dry horse," I laughed. We set about packing all our cases into the back of the Land Rover. Chris was carrying some of Maggie's belongings over.

"I 'ope you can get all this lot in. I told 'er she'd brought far too much stuff."

"Oh we'll manage. Just squash it all in somehow," I said. Maggie came over with the rest of her things and Chris went to help Allan transfer all Cammy's feed bags into the trailer. The wind was very blustery and blowing the vehicle doors. The horses were a bit jumpy as the wind kept whipping up their sheets. Eventually, everything was loaded up and it was time to tack up the horses. Danny-Boy's back was just about dry, thank goodness and I put the saddle on him quickly as Allan took his sheet and towel off. I went to get my brimmed hat in preference to my riding hat and pulled on my leggings. Chris was helping Allan to hang the horse sheets over the partition in the trailer. Maggie and I were almost ready to mount up when Joe and Carol arrived. Alf remained in the car with Carol but Joe came over to us, pulling his coat collar up round his neck.

"What have you done to the weather?" he asked grinning.

"It's all right for you, wrapped up nice and cosy in the Land Rover," I teased. "It's not too bad though and we've both got all our waterproofs on." Meanwhile, Chris was saying goodbye to Maggie, as he was leaving straight away and heading back to Rosedale.

"You'll be having a look in at market on t'way back Chris?" asked Allan.

"Well, I might 'ave ti stop a minute or two," he drawled, looking a little sheepishly at Maggie. She just laughed

"I didn't think you'd be able to drive through Hawes on market day without stopping. Well, don't go spending all our money," she said.

"I'll 'ave to see if there's owt at right price then," he chuckled, climbing into his vehicle. Soon he was gone, followed by Carol and her Dad, who were going to meet up with us at lunchtime. Joe got in with Allan and we were all ready to go. There was just a light rain but the wind was very gusty and as I climbed on Danny-Boy, he started prancing around, tossing his head, anxious to be off. David and Marie were standing huddled in their doorway, waving us goodbye.

"Thank you both for everything," I shouted, trying to make myself heard above the wind. As we set off down the road, I stood in my saddle to turn and wave a last goodbye. They were such kind people and I was truly grateful for all they had done for us. The horses were keen to go and we soon covered the mile on the busy main road before turning right, up the back road to Ingleton. We arrived in the village just before ten o'clock. Allan and Joe, who had overtaken us back on the main road, were parked up alongside a row of detached houses with neat well-kept gardens. As Maggie and I drew closer, we saw a grey-haired lady coming down her garden path to speak with them. Joe was explaining to her what we were doing when she approached the horses.

"What beautiful horses," she exclaimed. "Can I stroke them?"

"Yes, of course," I answered. "Do you like horses?"

"Oh, yes," she replied, patting their damp necks, gingerly. "I think they're wonderful creatures but I've never ridden one and I'm too old to start now," she laughed. "What is it you're collecting for? Leukaemia, did you say?"

"Yes, that's right," I replied.

"I'll go and get something for you." She turned and set off back up the path to the house. We stood on the pavement chatting while we waited.

"Must not be able to find her purse," suggested Joe, as we continued to wait. At last she re-appeared, struggling down the path with a bulging, black, bin-liner. We looked at one another in surprise.

"Hope it's not her life savings," Joe whispered in amusement.

"Here you are," she said, slightly out of breath. "I've been wondering who I could give these to. I hope they'll be useful. And good luck with the rest of your ride. Must go in now or I'll be getting wet." The rain was beginning to come down heavier and she smiled and waved as she turned and hurried back towards her house. Filled with curiosity, Allan and Joe were peering into the bag. Allan burst out laughing,

"Pans!" he exclaimed. "What are we going to do with these?"

"We'll have to take them," Joe replied. "She'll be offended if we leave them."

"Aye, you're right," added Allan. "Goodness knows where we're going to fit them in." Maggie and I were very amused at their predicament.

"She must have thought you two looked like a pair of tinkers," Maggie said, laughing. Allan was trying to squeeze the bag into the already overcrowded Land Rover.

"We'll be off then," I said, pulling the collar up on my coat, as the rain was now much heavier.

"We'll follow you through the village but I don't think there'll be many people about now with this weather," Allan remarked.

We made our way slowly through the village with the Land Rover following closely behind. Allan was right. There weren't many people around but ever hopeful, Joe kept jumping out and popping in and out of the shops where he saw customers. At the end of the main street we parted company. Maggie and I turned left and headed down towards the river. We paused a minute or two on the bridge, admiring the wonderful structure of the viaduct, carrying the railway line high above us. Maggie took a picture of the river flowing towards us on its way below the bridge. The banks were lined with trees of many types, heavy in leaf, and a few covered in blossom. The bank sides had been re-enforced with cobblestones, which seemed to sparkle as the water hurried over them. If only the sun had been shining.

Having crossed the bridge, we turned right and followed the river. The road soon left the riverside and we started to climb up away from the valley bottom. It was still raining steadily as we made our way up the steep, narrow road but we were sheltered from the wind by the trees growing on either side. When we reached the top of the hill, we left the trees behind and rode on, flanked on either side by stone walls.

"When do we get off these roads?" Maggie asked.

"Soon," I replied. "I bet these two are thinking it can't be too soon." We trotted on a while and at last reached a gate leading through to open pasture. We could now ride on the grass verge on the left of the road. There were sheep and lambs grazing on the short grass of the pastures, leading up to the foot of the sheer, rocky, limestone cliffs. We couldn't see the top of the crags because of the mist and rain but lower down a few stunted trees were trying to live in the shallow pockets of earth. Outcrops of rock dotted the pasture, becoming more prominent and larger as the ground rose higher.

On our right, looking over the wall, we could just see the main road running parallel to us, across the valley. The fell tops beyond were lost in the grey clouds of fog. We rode through several farmsteads, each separated from the next by a boundary wall with a gate across the road. Maggie and I took turns opening the gates, most of which swung easily but odd ones needed to be lifted.

"It looks a little brighter, Maggie. Maybe the rain's going to ease up a bit," I ventured. She laughed.

"I don't think so. The last time you said that, it came down even heavier. I'm already feeling damp down the back of my neck."

"I'm glad I put this hat on. I just keep tipping the water off! My hands are getting cold now, though."

"Mine are too," Maggie replied. "It's a pity no-one has invented a pair of really good waterproof gloves for riding, isn't it?"

"Yeah. I keep pushing one hand at a time under the saddle to warm it through. Look, that's our Land Rover over there, isn't it?" I queried, pointing over the valley.

"Yes, you're right. I bet they're in that roadside café having a nice hot cup of coffee!" We trotted most of the way up the valley as it helped to keep us all a bit warmer. Danny-Boy kept shaking his head, trying to prevent the rain from entering his ears. Tiny rivers of water were running down his neck from his soaking mane but, as usual, he appeared to be quite happy. Each farmyard we rode through seemed deserted. No one was around, just the occasional sheep-dog that barked as we passed through, letting us know people really did live there. Nestling under the towering crags, these farmsteads gave the impression of having been there for many years. At one farm, we saw an old 'fergy' tractor that I'm sure hadn't been started up for a very long time. I hadn't seen one of those since I was a child.

Eventually, we dropped down into the tiny hamlet of Chapel-le-Dale, at the top of the valley. It had seemed a long five miles since we left Ingleton. We passed the little chapel and graveyard among the trees, crossed over the bridge and rejoined the main road. The rain hadn't eased at all. In fact, it seemed to be even heavier as we trotted the last stretch of our morning's ride. The road was very busy with lots of heavy vehicles. Tankers, wagons, lorries and several huge cement mixers, along with speeding cars, all sending spray over us from the wet road. Not that we could get much wetter than we already were. Allan and Joe passed us, giving us an encouraging wave as they did so. At last, the familiar sight of the well-known landmark, the Ribblehead viaduct, came into sight.

"Thank goodness," said Maggie. "I can hardly feel my fingers."

"Ten minutes and we'll be there. I hope there's a fire on, even if it is the middle of May." The reins were cold and wet in my hands as I urged Danny-Boy on. "Come on, old fella, there's food waiting for you." He flicked one ear back, listening to my voice, and trotted resolutely on, with Cammy close behind, until we reached the welcoming haven of The Station Inn.

We rode round into the car park at the rear of the Inn, where Allan and Joe were waiting to help us. My hands and feet were numb as I slid down from my wet saddle.

"Are you leaving his saddle on?" Allan asked.

"Yeah, it'll help to keep him warm. Put his sheet over the top." Joe was helping Maggie with Cammy as Allan and I struggled with Danny-Boy's sheet. The rain was even heavier, coming down like stair-rods. I was just removing the bridle when a familiar voice spoke behind me.

"How's tha doing? Bit of a sod, this in't it?" I turned to see Laurie, his hood pulled over his head. Laurie had made arrangements for us to lunch here, as he knew the landlord. He had also provided him with one of my sponsor sheets so the landlord knew all about my ride.

"Aye, it is," Allan replied.

"Hi, Laur," I greeted him with a wry smile. "Couldn't be much worse, could it?" I turned to my husband who was fastening Danny-Boy's head-collar for me, as my fingers wouldn't work. "Al, what are we going to do with the horses? They can't stand out in this all the time while we're having lunch and the trailer's full of feed and stuff."

"No, you're right. We never expected having to use the trailer. We'll have to move some of it."

"A'll tell thee what," said Laurie. "Why don't thee shift all thi stuff into't back of my truck and then t'osses can stand int trailer?"

"Aye, we could do that," replied Al. "Shouldn't take us long. Why don't you and Maggie go on inside, Ann, while we see to it. Go and get warmed up. You must both be frozen. We'll see t'et horses and feed 'em." He took the lead rein from my hand.

"Okay, thanks," I replied, gratefully. "Come on Maggie," I called to her. She left Cammy with Joe and came over towards me.

"I'll just get her food ready, then I'll follow you in," she said, looking like a drowned rat with rain running down her face. I made my way round to the bar entrance and could hardly open the door, my hands were so cold. I tried to shake off some of the water from my clothes before entering. The warmth from a huge stove met me and the gentleman behind the bar smiled and greeted me as I walked in.

"Hello there, not the best of days, is it?"

"No," I replied, grinning. "I'm sorry about all this wet on your floor."

"Don't worry," he said, "we're used to that in here. Are you the lady doing the ride?" I suppose it wasn't obvious, me not wearing my riding hat.

"Yes, I am," I replied, smiling. I didn't feel much like a lady!

"You must be frozen. Hold on a minute and I'll get you a hot drink." He disappeared through a door into the back. I took off my dripping coat and hat and laid them over a chair near the stove. I was about to take off my leggings when Maggie came through the door.

"Oh, am I glad to see that," she said, approaching the stove. She, too, started to take off her wet clothing. When I removed my leggings, I found the rain had somehow got through and my jodhpurs were soaked, too. Just then the landlord returned with a steaming mug of hot coffee.

"Here, this will help to warm you up."

"Ooh, thanks," I said clasping both hands round the proffered mug. He gestured to Maggie.

"Is your friend riding with you?" he asked. I nodded.

"Yes, this is Maggie."

"Then she'll need a hot drink, too."

"Yes please." Maggie smiled her appreciation. She was still stripping off her clothes and found she was soaked right through to her tee shirt. The rain had run off her hat and down the back of her neck. Her coffee soon arrived and we stood huddled near the stove, sipping the hot liquid. My fingers were beginning to tingle as feeling began to creep back into them. A moment later Allan came through the door.

"What a flipping day!" he exclaimed. "We're just about soaked in that bit of time." Joe and Laurie were following him in. Laurie crossed to the bar to order some drinks.

"Are the horses okay?" I asked.

"Aye, they're both in the trailer with a hay-net. They've had their hand food," Allan answered.

"It's a good job Laurie showed up," said Maggie. "I wouldn't like to have left them out in this for long."

"No, they would soon have got starved." I hesitated a moment, then added, "Al, could I ask a favour of you?"

"Well, depends. Go on."

"Do you think you could go back outside into the Land Rover?" I smiled sweetly at him.

"You're joking, aren't you?"

"No, I wish I was. It's just that my breeches are wet through and Maggie's soaked to her shirt and we could do with some dry clothes from our cases. I'm sorry, do you mind?" I asked.

"No, of course not. You can't ride in wet clothes. Just tell me where to find them." We told him as best we could but with the Land Rover being as full as it was, it wasn't going to be an easy task. He turned and went back out into the pouring rain.

"It's very good of Allan. I feel awful sending him back out in this," Maggie said.

"What are you lasses having to eat?" Laurie had wandered over, a drink in his hand.

"We're still thawing out but I think hot soup and a sandwich would go down very well," I answered.

Carol and Alf had arrived earlier and had already ordered. They were sitting round the other side of the bar as the stove opened into both rooms. I was having a word with them when Allan returned with our dry clothes. Maggie and I thanked him very much and went off to change. By the time our lunch arrived, we were sitting by the stove feeling drier and much warmer. The soup was piping hot and I could feel it reaching almost to my toes. My hat was drying out near the stove and our other clothes were hung over chairs nearby. Looking out of the window at the rain still sheeting down outside, I thought how nice it would be to dally here an hour or too. But alas, not today.

We had almost finished lunch, when Joe, who had brought his collecting box in with him, jumped up.

"I'll just go and have a chat with the other customers," he announced cheerfully picking up his box. "We aren't going to see too many people around today." Several other people had taken refuge from the rain and were having lunch in the lounge end of the bar. I knew that we ought to be making a move, too, as we had a long, arduous ride ahead of us in the afternoon. It was warm and cosy as we all sat chatting and drinking our coffee. Laurie was puffing away on his faithful old pipe. Spirals of smoke drifted across the room leaving the pungent smell of tobacco in the air. I think we were all loath to leave the warmth and comfort that we were enjoying. I looked across at Maggie and smiled. Her face was glowing with the effects of the heat from the stove and the hot soup. Curls of still damp hair, now a deeper shade of copper, clung to the skin on her neck. I felt almost guilty as I spoke to her.

"It's almost one o'clock, we'll have to be on our way again."

"Yes, I know. I was hoping it might have stopped raining but it's still pouring down. Still, it can't get any worse," she said cheerfully. We started putting all our waterproofs back on while the men-folk settled the bill. Having thanked the landlord for his hospitality, we went out to face the rain again.

I entered the jockey door of the trailer to untie the horses and was met with a cloud of steam. At least that meant they were reasonably warm underneath their blankets. We fixed their bridles in the shelter of the trailer before backing them out and removing their sheets. After checking the girth, I was soon mounted and ready to start. Maggie quickly joined me.

"We'll see you down at the turn off," Allan called after us as we left the car park and headed down the road. It was still raining but not quite so heavily now. Unfortunately, the fog had become more dense and had dropped lower down the fell sides. We could just make out the impressive sight of the huge viaduct bridge that carries the main Settle to Carlisle railway line.

We were approaching the small road bridge over the stream at the bottom of the hill, when we heard a rumbling noise behind us. Turning our horses, we saw a freight train heading for the viaduct. Through the mist and fog we were just able to count its seventeen carriages as it disappeared eerily from our sight.

We continued on our way, trotting most of the time until we'd covered the two miles to where we had to turn off. Allan had overtaken us and had parked the Land Rover on the roadside. Joe jumped out and opened the gate for us.

"Thanks Joe, we'll see you in Hawes, I hope!"

"Don't get lost up there. It doesn't look too good."

"We'll try not to," laughed Maggie, as we made our way down the track to another gate. Once through, we headed towards the stream that we had to ford. Allan was standing on the footbridge with his camera waiting to see us across. What had been a shallow, moorland stream, meandering gently on its way on Sunday, was now a river in full spate. I approached the bank side, looking for a suitable place to cross. Danny-Boy was a little wary but dropped down into the water with a bit of encouragement from me. The current was quite strong and I felt his hind quarters sway as he moved into the middle of the steam. I kept him moving and we were soon on stony ground where the water was not so deep. I turned to see how Maggie was doing and was relieved to see Cammy following faithfully behind us. We climbed out on to the opposite bank and on to the track.

"A bit different from Sunday. You both did well," Allan called out.

"Yeah, I wasn't sure how deep it would be," I replied.

"Take care up there. We'll see you later, down near Hawes."

"Bye," we shouted in unison, as he waved from the bridge. We could barely see the Land Rover back on the road. We turned and started the long trek up the fell-side.

It was like riding into the unknown, and I was glad that I had my mobile phone with me. Fortunately, the path was a double track and well marked. The horses were refreshed after their rest and keen to go, so we trotted on until we reached the steepest part of the hill. Another track joined ours from the right, so I knew we were now on the Pennine Way. Here we walked until we reached the summit. Well, we presumed we had as the track levelled out considerably.

The fog was much thicker now and we could barely see five yards in front of us. It was still raining and the wind had risen, but fortunately it was driving the rain into our backs and right sides. Danny-Boy kept his face permanently averted keeping the rain from getting into his ears. Even though the track was comparatively level it had many potholes. They were full of water and we didn't know how deep they were, so this made trotting any great distance impossible. We couldn't leave the track, as the terrain on either side was boggy and dangerous. The horses were slipping about as it was so uneven, wet and greasy with all the rain.

Occasionally, we heard voices and then ghostly figures of walkers would loom into view from the mist. I felt sorry for them as they were facing the driving rain. Most of the time, Danny-Boy and I led the way and sometimes Maggie would get a bit behind and I would wait for her to catch up with me. Other times, I just called back to her rather than face the rain.

"Are you okay back there?" and I would get an instant response.

"Yes, we're fine." Where the track was better going, we'd ride alongside each other and have a little chat. Although the rain wasn't as heavy as it had been, it was still pretty cold and I was having to alternate my hands under the saddle to warm them. When we'd been riding about an hour we arrived at a fork in the track. The right one was sign-posted the Roman Road. Laurie had told us to keep left, which we did. I knew we were nearly halfway there but each mile we rode seemed more like two.

I didn't let my disappointment show but this was the day I had really been looking forward to. Away from all the traffic, high on the rooftop of England, I knew the views from up here must be spectacular. If only the fog and cloud would lift, just for a while, so that we could see far over to the mountains of Lakeland and to the moors and fells all around us. My imagination could not compare with the reality.

On we travelled, trotting wherever the terrain would allow, which wasn't often. I knew we were getting behind schedule but we couldn't go any quicker. An hour later we came to another fork where we again went left and through a gateway. The right track continued on the Pennine Way. Here we started to descend slowly and there was a fence on our left, beyond which we could just make out some forestry. As we descended, the track became steeper and more treacherous for the horses.

The track had been re-enforced with broken stones, presumably to make access for forestry vehicles. The stones were roughly hewn with sharp, jagged edges. It was impossible to find an alternate way down, as there was a high camber on the right of the track, with a deep gutter behind and beyond that, the steep hillside. On the left, the fence ran parallel to the track and only now and then could Danny-Boy climb on to the grassy base of the fence, as this was very narrow. I let him pick his own way, as it was impossible to choose a safe route for him. I hoped and prayed that he wouldn't trip or stumble because I daren't imagine what damage he could do to his knees.

I looked back to see that Maggie had dismounted and was leading Cammy down as best she could. Danny-Boy cautiously made his way over the smashed up stones, his shoes clattering against them with each step he took. Occasionally, he stepped up by the fence, whenever there was enough room.

Suddenly, I stopped and listened. Above the moaning of the wind in the trees, I was sure I could hear something.

"Maggie, listen! I'm sure I can hear traffic in the distance." She stood still, straining to hear above the noise of wind and rain.

"You're right," she replied. "We can't be that far from the road, now." We had reached the end of the forestry and looking ahead, we could make out

a gate across the track. We had apparently reached the end of the treacherous

section of our route.

"Thank goodness for that. I was terrified Cammy would stumble and go down with me on those awful stones," Maggie said. She was climbing back in the saddle after closing the gate behind us.

"It was pretty rough wasn't it?" Once through the gate, we discovered that we were on the open fell once more and so could pick our way a bit better. The track was not stony now but very muddy with deep ruts full of water. We continued to descend for about a mile before reaching another gate. This led us into a green lane where the track was hard and stony with muddy rivers of rainwater running down beneath our feet. We had almost reached the bottom of the steep fell side.

"We can't have far to go now. The traffic sounds much nearer." I said.

"The fog's beginning to clear a little," observed Maggie.

"Thank goodness. We're about an hour late. I hope they haven't been too worried about us. We'd better trot on a bit," I added.

"Okay." And then excitedly she exclaimed, "I can see vehicles down on the road. I was beginning to wonder if we'd ever see anyone again." It was certainly much clearer now and five minutes later the familiar sight of the Land Rover came into view, parked at the roadside. As we approached, Joe greeted us.

"Thought we were going to have to send a search party out for you two,"
he said. Allan was looking very relieved.

"We tried to contact you on the phone but couldn't get an answer. We thought something must have happened to you."

"No, we're both fine," I assured him. "It was pretty awful up there though and we couldn't rush at all. It was like being on some strange planet," I added. Maggie joined in.

"I thought we'd never get here. The track coming down was terrible. I had to get off and walk."

"We're glad you're both okay, anyway," said Allan.

"Well, we'd better push on now or everyone will have left the market!" I said.

"Aye, you're right," replied Al. "I'll drop Joe in the market place and go and park near the cattle mart." Maggie and I trotted down the last mile into Hawes.

"I can't believe it," said Maggie. " It's almost stopped raining!"

There were still plenty of people about and only a few stallholders were beginning to pack their wares away. We slowly made our way down the high street, with Joe and his box not far away. A few people were curious and most quite generous. The wind was gusty, blowing empty cartons and boxes around. One of these came flying right under Danny-Boy, making him shy a little but I think he was too tired to get too excited. We continued through the town, and did a tour of the car park before making our way to the cattle mart. There was a lot of traffic passing and some even stopped to give us their donations.

At last we were back at the trailer and Allan had the tailgate down ready. I untied my saddlebag, the contents of which were rather damp, and quickly removed the wet saddle and numnah. I took off Danny-Boy's bridle and fixed his head-collar while Allan put on the sheet. While we were attending to this, Carol and Alf arrived to collect Joe, for they were all going back home from here. Laurie arrived too, with his horse trailer. He was going to transport Cammy to save moving all the stuff out of our trailer again. He set about helping Maggie while Allan and I said goodbye to our good friends. Allan was going to miss Joe a lot, as he would be travelling all on his own from now on. We thanked Joe very much for all his hard work. He had done very well with the collecting box, taking over a hundred pounds over the two days. He said they hoped to meet up with us again later in the week but we were all a little sad as we waved them goodbye.

When both horses and tack were loaded up, I took off my waterproofs and hat and jumped in the Land Rover with Allan. Maggie got in with Laurie and we all set off for Laurie's home in Coverdale, where we would be spending the next two nights. I curled up in the Land Rover with Allan's warm dry coat wrapped round me. The heater was on full blast and I slowly began to feel warmer. I found my bottle of sherry from the day before and poured a drink into Allan's flask top. Yesterday evening seemed a lifetime away.

When we arrived at Laurie's, the skies were clearing and the fog had all but disappeared. Allan sent me straight in for a hot bath saying he would see to Danny-Boy. I promised Maggie not to be too long so that she could soon have one too. Linda met me at the door.

"I'll show you your room then you can have your bath. What an awful day it's been, hasn't it?"

"Yes, I hope tomorrow's a bit better."

"If you sort all your wet clothes out, I'll put them through the wash later. Dinner will be ready about six."

"Thanks Linda." I pulled off my boots in the back-kitchen and followed her upstairs. Clean towels were laid out ready and I was soon relaxing in wonderful hot water. By the time I got out, Allan had brought up our cases and I was soon dressed in jeans and sweater. As I left my room, I met Linda with more clean towels, followed closely by Maggie.

"I can't remember ever looking forward to a bath so much," she said, laughing.

"I'll see you later. I'm going to sort my tack out before dinner. Enjoy yourself !"

Linda's small back-kitchen seemed to be full of wet clothing, horse tack and boots. Having stripped off the wet numnah, I laid it on the pile of wet clothing that Allan had brought in, along with Maggie's saddle cover and numnah. I took my saddle over to Laurie's son, who lived close by, where there would be plenty of room. Andrew said he would put it out to dry the next day. I would have to use my spare one.

Soon we were all sitting around the large, oak, dining table in Linda's beautifully modernised kitchen. The roast beef and Yorkshire puddings went down very well with a glass of wine. Later, we sat by the glowing stove, drinking our coffee, Laurie puffing away at his pipe. He had organised a domino evening at his local pub to raise funds for our cause. As that was not until later, he invited Al to go for a look round his moor for an hour. Al accepted eagerly and off they went. Maggie and I helped Linda with the dishes, then I went for a lie down while Maggie went off to phone her family. I hadn't realised how tired I was and the wine had made me drowsy. I curled up on the bed and pulled the duvet half over me.

"Aren't you going out tonight?" Allan's voice startled me. I opened my eyes, for a moment not knowing where I was. He was getting dressed for the evening. Then I remembered.

"Gosh, is it late? I was sound off." He grinned at me.

"No, you're okay. It's just gone eight but you'll have to get changed now." I jumped off the bed.

"Did you have a nice ride out?" I asked, stretching my arms.

"Yes, it was lovely up on the moor. We saw quite a few broods of grouse chicks. I'll just go check on the horses while you get ready." He left the room.

Soon I was ready and went downstairs to join the others. Maggie was helping Linda to sort out raffle prizes and it wasn't long before we were all walking up the road to the pub. It was a lovely evening now. The sun was just going down behind the fell on the far side of the valley. Our horses were grazing contentedly in the field with

Darkie. Birds were singing in the trees and hedgerows as we walked along. How quickly the weather changes. It was like a different day.

The dominoes were well supported by the local people and the evening passed quite quickly. I was introduced to a young lady who had been diagnosed with Leukaemia a year earlier. Having undergone a course of treatment, she was now feeling fine and confident about the future. She wished to sponsor me and gave me a cheque saying how important it was to keep supporting the research. I thanked her very much and wished her all the best for the future. It was nearly midnight, when I asked Al if it would be okay for Maggie and I to leave. We slipped quietly away. The moon was high in the sky as we linked arms and wandered back through the quiet village. It had been a long, hard day and we were tired but happy. Two days completed and who knows what the morrow would bring?

The house was quiet and there was a smell of polish in the air. The stove was still glowing red and the table was laid ready for breakfast.

"Linda is so efficient, isn't she?" Maggie remarked.

"Yes, much better than I am. Look, all our washing has been done," I said, pointing to the old-fashioned pulley above the stove.

"Well, we can't be good at everything," she laughed. We went upstairs to bed. It seemed ages since we'd waved goodbye to Marie and David. I couldn't believe it was the same day!

"Goodnight Maggie, sleep well."

"You, too," she replied, as we hugged each other. "See you in the morning."

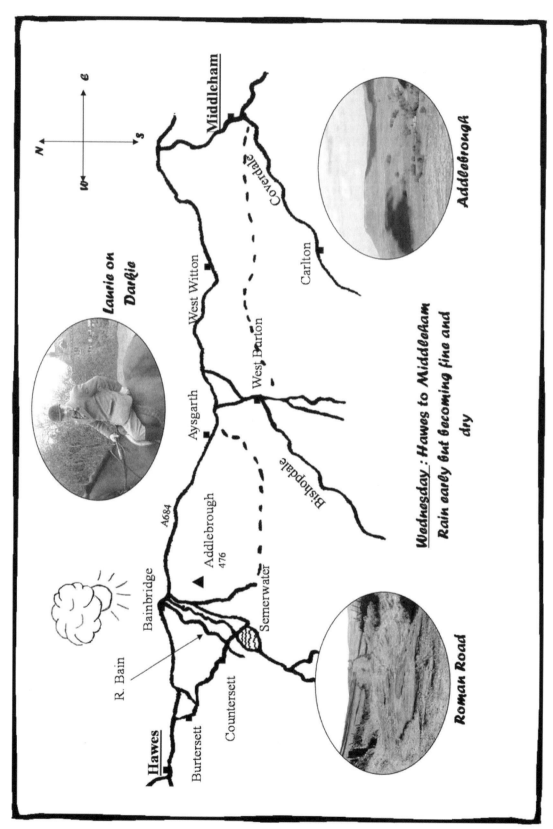

Hawes

Burtersett

Countersett

R. Bain

Bainbridge

▲ Addlebrough
476

A684

Semerwater

Roman Road

Bishopdale

West Barton

West Witton

Aysgarth

Coverdale

Carlton

Middleham

Lauria on Darfie

Addlebrough

Wednesday : Hawes to Middleham
Rain early but becoming fine and
dry

N   W   S   e

WEDNESDAY
MAY 24
HAWES TO
MIDDLEHAM.

I awoke early and crossed to the window. It was dull but at least I could see to the horizon on the far side of the valley. When I returned from the bathroom I woke Allan, who was sleeping soundly.

"C'mon sleepy-head, it's time to get up." He opened his eyes, a vague expression on his face.

"What day is it?" he asked.

"It's Wednesday and we have a long way to go. You must have come home late last night. I never heard a thing."

"Aye, you were sound off. Well, I'd better be up then," he said, sitting up in bed. "It's a fair way back to Hawes."

"I'll see you downstairs. Oh no," I said, glancing out of the window. "It's starting to rain again". At least Danny-Boy has his sheet on this time. I went down into the kitchen to find Linda busy cooking breakfast.

"Morning, Linda. Everyone okay?"

"Yes, fine thanks. Breakfast won't be long. Laurie's outside somewhere."

"Right, I'll go and bring Danny-Boy up for his feed." I took my coat from the back kitchen. "Can I borrow your wellies, Linda, please?" I shouted back through the doorway. I knew it would be easier to slip into them than pulling my riding boots on and off.

"She says yes you can." I turned to see Maggie standing in the doorway, smiling.

"Hi, I didn't know you were up and about." We were both soon outside and brought the horses into the yard from the paddock. We tethered them to the trailer and gave them their food. Darkie was already tied up near Laurie's trailer.

"Morning, girls. How's things?" Laurie greeted us as he emerged from a building.

"Okay, thanks," Maggie replied. "It's raining again."

"It's nowt this. It'll blow ovver afore long."

"Good, I hope you're right. Are you ready for your long ride?" I asked him.

"Ready as I'll ivver be. Might be a bit stiff ti'morrow tho'. I ain't ridden fer three months!" he laughed.

"Well, we'll just have to give you a good massage," Maggie teased. Having fed the horses we returned to the house where Allan was chatting to Linda and we were all soon tucking into a hearty breakfast.

"Quite a good turnout last night, wern't it?" said Laurie.

"Yes," I answered. "How much was raised then, Linda?"

"Almost a hundred pounds."

"Gosh, that was good. Thank you both very much for organising it all."

After breakfast, Maggie and I set about sorting out our tack, while Allan and Laurie went to remove all the contents of our trailer into Laurie's shed. As we were taking all three horses back to Hawes, we would need both trailers. Maggie's saddle was about dry, as it had been in the back kitchen but I had to use my spare one. It had almost stopped raining when we went to tack up the horses. I fixed my saddlebag after checking all the contents and fastened Danny-Boy's sheet over his saddle ready for the journey

Laurie's son, Andrew, was travelling to Hawes with his Dad to drive the vehicle back home. Maggie was going to travel with them, as there was more room in their truck than in our Land Rover. It was almost nine o'clock by the time we had all three horses loaded up and everyone was ready for off.

We arrived in Hawes to find the market place deserted, so there was plenty of room to park up the vehicles and unload the horses. They whinnied and called to each other as we backed them out of the trailer, each frightened they were going to be left behind. Soon we had removed the sheets and were all mounted ready to start. I tightened my girth, said cheerio to Al and followed Laurie and Maggie onto the main road. There was still dampness in the air but patches of blue were appearing in the sky.

We trotted a mile or so before turning right up a narrow lane, taking us through the tiny village of Burtersett. Dry stone walls ran either side of the road and divided the fields around us. Sheep and lambs grazed in many of the fields and every now and then there were old stone barns, some of which had seen better days. The wind had freshened and had blown the last of the rain away. Clouds chased across the sky, leaving large patches of blue where the sun was now breaking through.

We were steadily climbing as the road led us up the side of the fell. It was good to hear the birds again as we rode along, laughing and talking to each other. I saw meadow pipits and lapwings and heard a pair of curlews calling. Suddenly, I spotted a bird I didn't recognise.

"Laurie, what's that bird over there?"

"D'ye mean the oyster catchers?" he asked.

"No, I've seen those before. Those other two, there, look," I said pointing across the rough pasture on our left.

"Oh, I see. Them's Redshank," he replied. "Have you nivver seen them afore?"

"No. We don't have them on our moors. I see where they get their name from, though." Their long legs were bright scarlet.

"There's a few pair comes round these parts iv'ry year. Then they go again after't breeding time."

We crossed over the old Roman Road, continued climbing for a few more miles until we eventually started to descend. As we rounded a bend in the road, a wonderful view met our eyes. Far below, where the scurrying clouds were making a patchwork of shadows on the shimmering water, lay Semerwater. As we made our way down the narrow lane, more of the dale, lying west of the lake, came into view. A rectangular block of forestry lay nestled under the hillside at the head of the valley. Between this and the lake, farmsteads were dotted here and there among fields that stretched to the foot of the hillsides. A small stream, coming from high on the fell top, made its winding way down the centre of the valley into the lake.

"Looks beautiful today, doesn't it?" Maggie remarked.

"Yeah, sure does," I replied. "Does this valley have a name, Laurie?"

"Aye, it's called Raydale," he answered.

"We came here, many years ago, for a day out. There were people water-skiing on the lake and the children built castles in the sand and paddled in the shallow waters. We had a lovely time." For a while my mind returned to those halcyon days and I could picture all the four happy faces of my young family. I swallowed hard and quickly

brushed a silent tear from my face. We trotted through the tiny hamlet of Countersett and down towards a strong, stone built bridge with v-shaped alcoves, which spanned the stream.

"This is the river Bain," said Laurie as we paused a moment. "It is the shortest river in the country."

"Really?" remarked Maggie. "How come?"

"Well, it only runs from the lake, down through Bainbridge and into the River Ure."

A pair of ducks flew off at the sound of the horses' hooves clattering over the bridge. I noticed a water-hen swimming quietly out of sight among the undergrowth by the river's edge. Allan had parked the Land Rover by the roadside, near the lake and was out with the camcorder as we approached.

"Take them into the water," he shouted to us.

"Good idea," said Maggie.

"Aye, they'll enjoy cooling off their feet," said Laurie.

How good it was to be off the hard road as we walked over the shingle and soft sand to the lakeside. Danny-Boy splashed into the water and we waded out until the water was knee-high. He bent to drink and snorted as the mini waves broke on his nose. Laurie was pushing further out into deeper water.

"I wonder if Darkie 'ed swim if I went out fother?" he grinned back at us.

"You try," shouted Maggie laughing. "This is as far as I'm going." Suddenly, Danny-Boy's head shot up. He'd heard voices over to our left. Turning him towards the sound, I rode ahead and, round the corner of some

bushes, saw a party of school children by the side of the lake. They were certainly enjoying themselves from the laughter that I could hear. I turned back and followed the other two across the shallow water of the lake, letting Danny-Boy have one more drink before leaving the lakeside. It would have been nice to have lingered a while and I'm sure the horses would have liked that, too, but we had to press on.

We were soon on our way, climbing up the road from the lakeside. We travelled about half a mile before taking a sharp, left hand turn back down the side of the valley. The fell side rose sharply on our right and now and then, little streams hurried down the steep hillside through the rocks and stones. Deep crevices and gullies had formed over the years, caused by swollen streams after heavy rainfalls. There was no sign of any rain now and the clouds were few and scattered.

We were all feeling rather warm and had removed our raincoats. I had stuffed mine into my saddlebag. Maggie had tied hers round her waist.

"I hope Mr. Bowes is waiting up front for us. I think we could do without all these waterproofs," declared Laurie. Thankfully, as we trotted round the next bend, we saw the familiar Land Rover parked near a farmyard. We all dismounted, removed our leggings and handed the whole lot to Allan.

"Good job you waited, Al," I said.

"I wasn't sure where you would be climbing out," he answered.

"There's no bridleway ovver this part," Laurie informed him. "We have ti travel almost ti Bainbridge and then cut back again before we can tek t't fells." Feeling much freer, we trotted on briskly to the next junction and, as Laurie had described, took a sharp right turn and started climbing steeply up the narrow lane.

The bleak, barren form of Addlebrough rose high on our left. The only vegetation was the short, stunted grass providing a meagre existence for hardy sheep. I could imagine how wild and wind-swept it would be in the wintertime. The solid stone walls provided the only form of shelter for the tough moorland sheep grazing here.

After a couple of miles, we reached the end of the hard road, at the last farmstead. Passing quietly through, we turned left through a gateway and began to climb yet again. It was great to be off the tarmac and feel soft earth beneath our feet, even if it was a bit boggy in places. As we climbed higher, the terrain became much stonier where the surrounding earth had been slowly eroded away over hundreds of years. Although most of the stones were covered in moss and scrubby grass, the horses still had to pick their way carefully.

It was wonderful up on those fell tops. The air was clean and fresh, the light breeze preventing it being too hot for the horses. How they enjoyed it up there, vying to keep up with one another and no traffic to bother about. The views were fantastic. We could see for miles, right across the expanse of Wensleydale and the moors beyond. Looking behind us, we could see way back, west of Hawes. We had no need to say much. I felt in awe of the sheer joy I felt, riding on Danny-Boy up here in a world that seemed totally ours. I felt at one with nature and revelled in the feeling of absolute isolation from the rest of the world. If it rained for the rest of the week, I would always have this day for which to be grateful. Laurie seemed to know where he was leading us as we picked our way over the rough terrain. We passed brokendown stone walls and gateways where gates no longer hung. He pointed out landmarks and informed us where each track we passed led to. I was grateful that he was with us.

All too soon, we started to descend and fields appeared in the distance. Laurie had found the track that would eventually lead down to Aysgarth. A mile further on and we were trotting on a track down the side of a grass field.

"C'mon," shouted Laurie. "Lets have a canter down here."

"Cammy's a bit tired," Maggie replied. "You go on. I'll just trot on behind." I let Danny-Boy follow Darkie down the field side, his head tossing in sheer delight. I was thinking of all the miles we had to do in the afternoon and thought maybe that I should have held him back but he was enjoying himself too much. We had cantered a hundred yards or so when he became more exuberant than ever. He was bouncing about and every now and then kept kicking his back legs out. Suddenly, I heard Maggie shouting excitedly behind me but couldn't understand what she was saying. I tried to pull Danny-Boy up but he was determined to catch up with Darkie, bucking and jumping about as we went. Eventually, as we caught up with Darkie, I drew him to a halt but he seemed agitated. Laurie was laughing his head off.

"Quite a performance that, Mrs. Bowes," he remarked. Maggie came trotting up and exclaimed, with a big grin on her face,

"You've bust your saddlebag."

Looking down, I saw the saddlebag swinging loose underneath my startled horse. I jumped off quickly. One side had broken away from where it had been attached to the saddle and the whole lot had swung over the top. No wonder Danny-Boy had been creating.

"I thought you were going to end up on the grass," Maggie said, laughing at me.

"I wasn't too sure, myself! I had to keep my heels hard down. I'd better check and see what's missing." I soon discovered I'd lost my phone, my penknife and my lip salve. Taking some string from the other side of my bag that was still intact, and borrowing a knife from Laurie, I did a temporary repair job on my saddlebag. We spent the next ten minutes walking back up the field searching for my lost possessions. Luckily, we managed to find everything and were soon mounted and on our way.

Half a mile further down the track we came across a herd of suckler cows with their young calves. They had wandered from their field on to the track and looked as if they hadn't seen riders before. We walked quietly in single file, hoping they wouldn't stampede. They kept galloping along in front of us, making quite a commotion, but eventually the track widened out and they veered off up another field, none the worse for their encounter.

Soon, we were trotting down the last stretch towards an open gate that led to the main road.

"Ooh, look, there's that man again," joked Maggie as she spotted Al with his camcorder resting on top of the wall. He smiled as we rode up to him.

"Everything all right?" he asked.

"Yeay, we had a great ride over the fell," I replied, beaming back at him.

"Had a bit of excitement coming down't fields," Laurie laughed. "Ann was showing off her rodeo skills!" We went on to tell him of my mishap. Al just laughed, saying,

"I should have had my camera there." We continued on our way and Allan passed us on the main road as we trotted down into Aysgarth. He had the water buckets filled ready when we arrived at the car park of the George and Dragon.

The horses enjoyed their drink as we tethered them to the trailer and gave them a small ration of hand food. I loosened the girth on my saddle to let Danny-Boy's back cool down and when they'd eaten their hand food, we tied the hay-nets to the back of the trailer. Satisfied that they were all okay, we went inside for a much needed drink. I remembered to take along my collecting box and placed it on the end of the bar. The landlord knew of our arrival, as Laurie had booked us in earlier.

We were soon enjoying our soup and sandwiches and Allan was busy chatting to a pair of gentlemen who seemed very interested in our ride. They were even more delighted to chat to him when they found out where we were from, as they had holidayed many times in Rosedale in years gone by. They spent our lunchtime reminiscing about people whom they'd all known.

Over lunch, Maggie told me that she thought it would be a good idea if she rested Cammy that afternoon. The previous day's ride had taken a lot out of the old horse and we had ridden many miles that morning. As I would have Laurie riding with me, she felt she wouldn't be letting me down too much. I assured her that it would be fine, as I knew she desperately wanted to complete the rest of the journey. As I took my collecting box round the customers, Maggie asked Allan if he minded taking Cammy back to Laurie's in the trailer while we rode on to Middleham.

After lunch, we helped Allan tidy up the car park and load Cammy into the trailer before Laurie and I set off down the road. Danny-Boy seemed rather despondent as we trotted along and I asked Laurie to follow me awhile to see if he was sound. I just felt that he wasn't going like his usual self.

"He's not lame at all," said Laurie.

"Maybe he's just sulking a bit because Cammy isn't with us," I suggested. We left the main road and turned off down to the village of West Burton. We turned left over an old packhorse bridge and up a cart track leading to a couple of farms. At the second farm we came across a lost lamb bleating for its mother. Laurie was able to get ahead of it and we managed to turn it into the farmyard where we hoped it would be tended to.

We continued climbing steeply on the well-marked grassy track that eventually levelled out high on the side of the fell. Danny-Boy seemed much happier now and trotted freely alongside Darkie. It was a glorious afternoon and the views were again spectacular. We could see far down the valley towards Leyburn and beyond as we trotted along the side of the fell. The stark outline of Penhill towered above us on the right. There was more vegetation here in the lee of the fell side. Trees and shrubs robed in green edged the fields and sheep and lambs grazed contentedly, happy to have the warm sun on their backs after the previous day's rain. Below us on our left, tractors were busy in the fields and there were cows again lying peacefully, chewing their cud.

After a few miles, we reached the hard road above the village of West Witton and turned right. Here the road ascended steeply and at the top we turned left-handed on to the road leading past the High Moor of Middleham. I saw for the first time the amazing all weather training gallops. I couldn't believe it was possible to find such a perfectly flat area of land so high up. Laurie explained that the circular track was five miles long.

"C'mon, let's try 'er out," he invited, grinning cheekily.

"No, I'm not," I replied, laughing. "It's all right for you, but my horse has another four days riding to do."

"Well, me an' Darkie's gonna have a go!" He set off down the middle of that superb track at a fair gallop. Danny-Boy was hanching at his bit, desperately asking to follow but I held him to a trot. Laurie must have gone half a mile or more when he suddenly pulled up and turning, shouted something back to me. I couldn't make out what he said and Laurie was now trotting back to me. As he neared me, I noticed a very worried look on his face.

"Have you seen anything of mi pipe? I lost the damn thing out o' mi pocket."

"I never saw a thing," I replied. His concern was growing. To Laurie, life without his pipe just didn't bear thinking about.

"I'll atty find it. It's t'only one I 'ave and it's half day closing. I can't git another 'til ti'morrow," he groaned.

"I'll help you look for it. I'll start here, you go back to the start," I suggested. He again set off at a gallop, back to where we'd entered the track and I started slowly retracing our steps, closely surveying the ground as I went. Suddenly there was a whoop of delight. I looked up and saw a jubilant Laurie waving his hand in the air, holding the treasured pipe. He came trotting up to me, a huge grin on his face.

"By gum, but I were lucky there. I thought we might be looking rest et day." He put the beloved pipe in a secure pocket and added, "Right, we'll 'ave another go, Darkie." He gathered his reins and with one squeeze of his legs was away.

I smiled to myself as he again set off at full speed down the track. I saw him pull up in the distance and turn around. We both arrived at the exit gate together and trotted along the hard road once more until we reached the Low Moor gallops.

These are almost as impressive as the others, such a vast area of flat, green grass. It must seem like paradise to the racehorse trainers. No wonder there are so many of them around Middleham. The bridleway runs across these gallops and we soon trotted the mile or so down towards Middleham. Suddenly, I spotted the familiar red banners on our trailer across the gallop.

"Look, Laur, there's Al over there."

"C'mon then, I'll race you back," he challenged. This time I let Danny-Boy have his head and we cantered towards the trailer. Danny-Boy whinnied when he saw it, thinking his mate would be there. It was good to feel the wind in my face and the power beneath me as we raced across the hallowed turf.

"He's not tired then?" asked Allan, as we pulled up by the trailer.

"No, he really enjoyed that but I daren't let him overdo it. I have to think of tomorrow," I replied, a little breathlessly. "It's been a smashing afternoon, hasn't it? Did you get Cammy back okay?"

"Yes. The rest will have done her good. I think Maggie was a bit disappointed, though." We soon had the tack off both horses and loaded them into the trailer. It was a bit of a squash in the Land Rover but it was only a twenty-minute journey back to Carlton where Laurie lived.

"Bags I have first bath tonight Mrs. Bowes. I've a feeling I might be a bit stiff in the morning," declared Laurie as we made our way through narrow country lanes.

"You could always take Maggie up on her offer," I teased.

"Aye, well there's a thought," he chuckled. "I've a feeling the missus might have sommat to say about that!"

"Thanks for today, anyway, Laur. It's been wonderful. I would never have found my way over those fells. We were so lucky with the weather, too." Soon we were pulling into Laurie's yard. Maggie waved when she saw us, a big smile on her face. She was sitting out in the sunshine, cleaning her tack. She came over and helped unload the horses. They had sweated up a bit in the trailer.

"Best bring him down to the stable, Ann and we'll hose them down," Laurie suggested. His stable was a hundred yards down the village. I agreed with him and so we led them both down the road and gave each of them a good hosing on their legs. Afterwards, I led Danny-Boy back to the house and tied him to the trailer to eat his hand food while I towelled him down. I then sheeted him up and turned him loose in the field with Cammy. As I returned, I noticed my other saddle on the fence by Andrew's house and went across to collect it. Ann, Andrew's wife, came out of the house with a toddler in her arms.

"Hi, your saddle should be dry now," she smiled at me. "Have you had a good day?"

"Yes, great, thanks. Is this young Dan?" I asked, walking over towards them. Although the youngster was a year old, I hadn't seen him before.

"Yes. I'm just going to give him his tea. Would you like to come in for a coffee or are you keen to have your bath?" she asked.

"I'm second in the queue," I grinned at her. "Laurie insisted on first bath, so I'd love to have a drink with you."

"You can have a bath at our house. Then Laurie won't have to rush."

"Sounds like a good idea. Thankyou. I'll just go and get my things." After I'd put my saddle in the Land Rover, I returned to get what I needed from my bedroom and tell Linda of my plan.

"She's gone down to find Laurie with a phone message," Maggie informed me. She was busy writing postcards to send home.

"Gosh, that reminds me. I must go and phone Sara. Little Josie is five today and I promised to wish her happy birthday." I stayed and chatted a while then went upstairs to make my call and collect my things.

It had been a long day in the saddle and I really appreciated my bath. We were all going out for a meal but not 'til later so I had time to wash and set my hair. I even had time for a play with young Dan before his bedtime. Soon after, Andrew returned home from work so I took my leave of them.

When I entered the house, I found Laurie and Allan sitting by the stove having a leisurely chat discussing the prospects of the forthcoming grouse season. Smoke was circling from the much-loved pipe. I smiled to myself, thinking of what might have been. Linda was busy, as usual, finishing off a large stack of ironing. I thanked her very much for doing all our washing as she handed me a pile of clean laundry. I then went upstairs, hoping to find Maggie who had been having a rest. I hadn't been in my room a minute when there was a knock on my door.

"Can I come in?" Maggie stood beaming outside our bedroom.

"Yes, of course. I was just coming to wake you." We discussed the evening ahead and what we should wear, as girls do. We were treating Laurie and Linda to dinner and had arranged to return to The George and Dragon in Aysgarth. Presently we heard the others coming upstairs and decided we'd better be getting ready.

We all enjoyed an excellent meal accompanied by more than the odd glass of wine. It was just gone midnight when we arrived back home and I was more than ready for a good night's sleep.

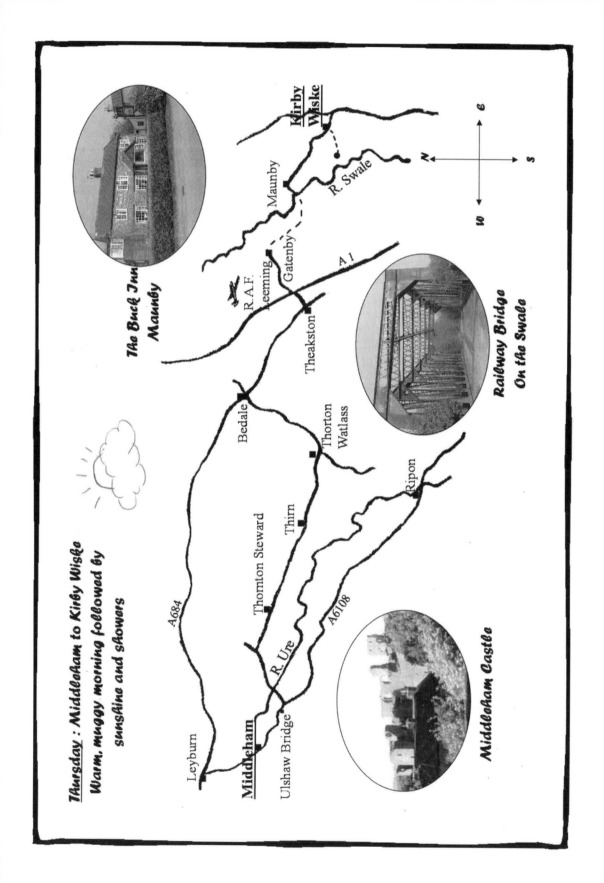

Thursday : Middleham to Kirby Wiske
Warm, muggy morning followed by sunshine and showers

The Buck Inn
Maunby

Railway Bridge
On the Swale

Middleham Castle

THURSDAY MAY 25
MIDDLEHAM TO
KIRBY WISKE

I rose early and was searching through my case for a clean pair of jodhpurs, when I realised the week was already half gone. Amazingly, I thought, tomorrow night I would be sleeping in my own bed. However there were still a lot of miles to ride between here and Fryup. I woke Al before going downstairs and having pulled Linda's wellies on, went to fetch Danny-Boy. Maggie was already outside getting Cammy's food ready.

"Hi, I didn't know you were up. Did you sleep okay?" I asked her smiling.

"Yeay, like a log. I hope Cammy has rested up, too."

"I'm sure she'll be fine. I think you did right yesterday. It was a long day. Lets go and see how they are." We picked up their lead ropes and walked over to the gate into the field. The horses were all at the far end and their heads shot up when we shouted. Danny-Boy gave an answering whinny and set off up the field towards us at a canter with Cammy in hot pursuit.

"There's your answer," I said laughing. "I don't think there's much wrong with those two." It took us a while to extricate them from the field without letting Darkie out. Eventually, we had them tethered near the trailer and left them tucking into their breakfast. We returned to the house for ours and found everyone else up and about.

After breakfast, Maggie and I went upstairs to pack, while Al went out to start moving all the gear back into the trailer. Laurie had offered to transport Cammy in his trailer, back to the gallops where he and I had finished riding the day before. This was a great help, as there would be just room for Danny-Boy in our trailer after all the bags of horse feed, barrels of fresh water, buckets and the rest of the tackle had been reloaded.

Having brought our cases down, Maggie and I went out to get the horses ready. Although the morning was dull and overcast, at least it was dry and we could give them a good brush down. As usual, I checked Danny-Boy's legs for any bumps or swelling but he was fine. When I had brushed out his mane and tail, he looked really smart again. I found a clean numnah and saddled him up with my old saddle. I put on his bridle with the head-collar over the top and sheeted him up ready for the journey.

While I had been busy with Danny-Boy, Laurie had been helping Maggie load Cammy up and Allan had managed to squeeze everything into the Land Rover. He walked round to me, just as I was leading Danny-Boy into the trailer and closed the tailgate for me.

"Are you having a quick coffee before we go?" called Laurie.

"Good idea," said Al.

"I don't think I will. What about you Maggie?" I asked.

"No thanks, but we'll come and say goodbye to Linda."

We all returned to the house where Linda had the kettle boiling. Words were inadequate in thanking them for all they had done for us but, as old friends do, they knew how much we appreciated their help and hospitality. At last, we were ready to go and after popping in to say a quick goodbye to Ann and baby Dan, we were pulling out of the yard and taking the road back to the gallops.

We parked the vehicles on the grass near the hard road alongside the gallops and began to unbox the horses. Cammy suddenly started to get very excited and whinnied loudly. She had seen the string of race-horses trotting towards us as they returned from their morning exercise. Maggie was hanging on to her as she danced around.

"I thought for a minute she was going to join them, Maggie," I said, as the string disappeared towards Middleham.

"I'm sure that's what she had in mind," laughed Maggie. After removing the sheets and head collars, we mounted up and set off down the road. Both horses seemed on their toes and we soon trotted the mile or so into Middleham. The sound of metal shoes on stone echoed through the air as we made our way across the cobbled area in the centre of the town. Richard Wells, a reporter from the B.B.C. was there to greet us, accompanied by another man, whom Richard introduced to us as the chairman of the Middleham Jockey Club. This gentleman chatted about our ride, then handed me a cheque for fifty

171

pounds, explaining that the jockeys had donated it.

"That's most generous of them. Thank you. I hope you will pass on my appreciation," I said.

"I will. Some of them would like to have ridden along so far with you but, as you can see, this is a very busy time of day for them."

As we were speaking, more strings of horses were passing through the square. Some were coming from the gallops and others were on their way to exercise. Quite a few waved and shouted to us as they rode through. They would realize who we were from our tabards. Danny-Boy and Cammy were behaving very well, standing quietly. Richard owned a horse so was very interested in ours and asked about their breeding and what training had been necessary for our ride.

Laurie returned from his tour round the town centre and I smiled to myself as I noticed his gait wasn't quite as relaxed as usual! Never mind, his stiffness would wear off in a day or two. We chatted a while longer, and then it was time to start our day's ride. Laurie gave his collecting box to Allan and was puffing away on the old pipe as we said our goodbyes.

It was ten o'clock when we set off down the main road, which would eventually lead us to Bedale. It would be a long ride of eleven miles and all on the hard road. As we were leaving the outskirts of Middleham, we passed some racehorse stables where they had one of those horse walkers. It rather startled Danny-Boy, as it was just over the wall behind the pavement. He soon relaxed and both horses settled down into a rhythmic trot. About a mile and a half further down the road, we turned left at the bridge over the river Ure at

Ulshaw. Seeing the lovely old church, standing there solitary among the trees, took my mind back to when we lived in Wensleydale, as this was the church we used to attend.

Down here in the valley bottom, the stone walls had given way to leafy hedgerows. The fields were lush and green. Here and there the first cuts of grass had been made and the familiar black and white of the Friesian milk herds were to be seen again. There were fewer sheep and more land was given to arable crops. There was little traffic on this quiet country road and we had just the singing and whistling of the birds to accompany us as we trotted mile after mile.

There was very little breeze and the air was close and sticky. Danny-Boy seemed very sluggish and even surrendered his leading role to Cammy. For the first time, I began to question his endurance. I desperately wanted to complete the whole week on him. It was increasingly hard work, having to encourage him all the time and as we passed each signpost, every mile seemed longer than the previous one. I voiced my concern to Maggie.

"Maybe he's just bored. It does get a bit monotonous for them, mile after mile on the hard road, especially after yesterday," she suggested.

"Maybe. I hope there's nothing wrong. We're only halfway through our ride."

"Perhaps he needs a higher energy food. You could try him with some of Cammy's 'super plus' at lunchtime and see if it makes any difference."

"Yeay, okay. I'll do that." We continued on, occasionally walking but mostly trotting, passing through the villages of Thornton Steward, Rookwith, Thirn and Thornton Watlass. Where the grass verge was wide enough, we encouraged the horses to use it and give their legs a break from the constant pounding of the hard roads. A couple of miles from Bedale, the weather changed. The air became much cooler and dark clouds appeared in the distance, which seemed to be heading our way. As we neared Bedale, there was a noticeable increase of traffic and the high street itself was very busy as we entered the town.

"Where is Mary going to be?" asked Maggie.

"I'm not sure. I just know it's in front of the pet shop," I answered, as we cautiously made our way up the main street. Maggie suddenly pointed ahead.

"Look, Ann, over there." I followed her gaze and saw a huge banner, strung high up between two posts. Big smiles spread over our faces.

"Typical Mary!" I exclaimed. On the banner in bright red letters was written 'Welcome, Danny-Boy'. Allan was parked alongside in the allotted space the police had allowed him and there, grinning up at us, was Mary.

"Well done lasses. Would you like a drink? Where are the other riders?" she asked.

"What other riders," I queried, jumping down from my horse and embracing my dear friend.

"The girls who are going with you this afternoon. They went to meet you."

"We've never seen any riders," Maggie added. She, too, had

dismounted and I introduced her to Mary.

"Oh well, never mind. I'll go and find them. You must have come in a different way. Look, there are some sandwiches for you here and plenty to drink. See you later." She jumped into her car and drove off in search of her friends.

Almost immediately, the heavens opened and it was freezing cold with it. We grabbed the sheets from the trailer and quickly threw them over the horses then we sheltered in the trailer while we ate the sandwiches. The poor horses just stood, heads hung down with rain running down their necks and faces. No one needed to hold them, it was plain to see that they weren't going anywhere.

Another lady, Pat, who was a supporter from the local branch of the L.R.F. had come to help with the collecting. She had dashed into the Pet shop until the rain subsided. While we were in the trailer, we sorted out the food for the horses and Allan filled the water bucket in readiness. By the time Mary returned, having located her friends, the shower had eased and we were feeding the horses.

"Right, where's another collecting box? C'mon Ann, we're going on a pub crawl. Are you all right with the horses Allan?" she asked. Maggie had already gone off down the street, as she wanted to buy some small gifts for her children.

"Aye, I'll be fine. Don't get Ann drunk, will you?" he joked. "I don't know if you can be breathalysed on a horse."

"We haven't time to drink anything," Mary retaliated, laughing. "Plenty of time for that tonight." I had donned my waterproofs while in the trailer, as it was still raining and we set off up one side of the main street. I had never realised just how many public houses there are in the towns. Having crossed the busy road at the bottom of the high street, we made our way back up the other side. We must have been in seven or eight establishments and in each one our reception varied. Some were very pleasant and the customers responded generously, while others were very different, where only one or two old soaks adorned the bar, giving us very funny looks.

"Oh, well, never mind," said Mary cheerfully. "You can't win 'em all." We hastily retreated from such places and continued on our quest. Eventually, we made our way back to the Land Rover. Pat, having left the shelter of the Pet shop, had been doing her best in the rain to catch the attention of passers by. One of these had taken pity on our horses and given them a carrot to eat.

On our excursion round the town, I had noticed a branch of the bank I use and decided to deposit most of the cash we had collected so far. I felt rather vulnerable as I hurried quickly down the street with my box of cash and paying-in book, as I was carrying several hundred pounds. I felt relieved as I handed it all over the counter. The cashier was not too happy at having to count out all the assortment of notes and coins but grudgingly accepted it all and I was soon back with the others.

Maggie had returned with her shopping and the other girls on horseback had just arrived, so Maggie and I set about getting ready to join them. I had met a couple of the girls on one of my visits to Mary's home. We were soon all introduced and eager to start. As usual, Allan was left tidying up the sheets and food with Mary. We wouldn't see them again until we reached Maunby.

"Good luck, girls!" Mary shouted after us, as we set off down the busy main street. "I hope you get through okay." I hoped so, too. This was the section of the route that had caused all the problems. Once out of town, we put the horses to a trot on the road leading to Exelby. The rain had eased considerably, although Maggie and I kept our waterproofs on.

I don't know if it was the different food that I had given Danny-Boy or the presence of other riders, but he was a different horse from the morning. He took over the leading role and with head held high, set off at a fair pace down the road. Maybe he was just showing off, or maybe letting the other horses know who was in charge of *this* herd of horses. I had to keep bringing him back to a walk to let the other riders catch up.

As we approached the village, one of our friends declared that she would have to pay a call at the local pub. When we arrived, a touring bus was in the car park and appeared to have a problem.

"Just a flat tyre," explained the driver in answer to our queries, as he continued his repair job. "My customers didn't mind. They're all inside having some refreshment."

"I'll go and say 'hello' to them," volunteered one of the girls. "They might have a collection for you, Ann." Two of them dismounted and went inside while we held their horses. Presently, the driver, having fixed the tyre, went to inform his charges. The girls returned and passed me handfuls of change that they had collected. Eventually, all the passengers, most of whom were pensioners, came trooping out. Smiling cheerfully, they came over to see the horses and have a chat with us. I thanked them all for their kindness and we waved them goodbye as they all climbed back into their bus.

A mile further down the road, we came across a Land Rover parked on the grass verge with a lady standing next to it.

"This will be the owner of the stud farm," one of the girls informed us. "She said she'd be waiting here." The said lady was opening the gate into the lane.

"Thank you very much for allowing us to pass through your farm," I smiled at her. Mary had told me she had been very reluctant to let us through at the first time of asking, but had later relented. She was frightened that our horses might upset her mares and foals.

"I have opened the padlock on the boundary gate onto the flyover. I'll come down later to lock it again. Please ride through as quietly as possible," was her parting request. We all set off down the lane at a gentle pace. There was a high, thick hedge on our left and post and rail fencing on the other side. We chatted and talked to each other as we rode quietly along and never even saw a horse. Soon we could hear the roar of traffic and arrived at the unlocked gate taking us on to the flyover that crossed above the A1. We trotted quickly over and Danny-Boy was much more relaxed this time. We closed the gate on the far side and trotted on to meet our next hurdle. The Airfield.

I was trying to stay relaxed to prevent Danny-Boy becoming apprehensive. We had almost drawn level with the entrance to the R.A.F. base, when the inevitable happened. A deafening roar filled our ears as a jet began to take off. The noise was horrendous and soon we could see the huge aircraft taking to the sky. Amazingly, Danny-Boy hardly flinched. I think it was his stallion instincts coming to the fore and showing a good example to his herd. I was the one giving a big sigh of relief.

On we went, past the airfield to the little village of Gattenby, where we left the hard road and took to the fields. From now on, I was in the hands of our friends. We passed through a couple of fields and reached the embankment on the river Swale. These banks, which are as wide as a road, are very high to prevent flooding of the flat surrounding fields and Danny-Boy became very excited. He was bouncing around and would love to have galloped off down to the next gate each time.

To our immense relief, all the boundary gates had been unlocked and we made it safely through to the old metal, disused railway bridge which spanned the river. The bridge echoed loudly as we all clattered over it and there greeting us on the other side were Mary and Allan. I was very pleased to see them. We had surmounted all our obstacles without mishap and all had a good ride together. Even the sun came out as we trotted the last half-mile into the village, where the girls had their horseboxes.

Mary was waiting in the pub car park, waving us in like a marshal at a pit-stop.

"C'mon, drinks are on me. What would you all like?" As I was desperate to pay a call, I went inside with Mary and helped carry all the drinks out to the others. It was a very happy, relaxing ten minutes. Maggie and I again removed our waterproofs, as it was now quite warm with no threatening clouds in the sky.

"I don't think we'll need them any more today," I said, handing them all to Allan.

"No, it's turned out grand, hasn't it?" he replied. Later, Mary collected all the glasses, while Maggie and I mounted up once more. The other girls were setting off back to their boxes in the village.

"Thank you for everything. We could never have done it without your help," I told them.

"You're welcome. We've all had a good ride out and are glad we were able to do our bit for you," replied Sue, one of the girls I'd met on my visit to Mary's. "We may see you again this evening," she added.

"Great," I shouted after them as they trotted off. Mary returned from taking all the glasses back and walked over to us, patting Danny-

Boy as she spoke.

"You know your way from here. Just turn right at the end of the village and you'll be on the road to Kirby Wiske," she informed us, before walking back to her car.

Maggie and I set off once more, making our way through the quiet little village of Maunby and were soon trotting on the road towards Kirby Wiske. Allan and Mary had overtaken us back in the village.

"Danny-Boy seems to have settled down now," remarked Maggie.

"Yeay, good job too. I was having a struggle with him along the embankments. I think he was just showing off to the other horses."

"They were a grand bunch of girls, weren't they? It was good of them to come all the way with us."

"Yes, we would probably have got lost on our own," I replied. We could see the village ahead of us now.

"How far is it to Mary's farm?" Maggie asked.

"Oh, less than a mile from the village, I think. We should be there before four o'clock." It was a lovely afternoon now. The sun was shining and a gentle breeze was blowing, making it very pleasant as we trotted along. As we approached the sleepy little village of Kirby Wiske, a family of ducks appeared from a gap in the hedge and waddled in single file across the road in front of us. They simply ignored the horses.

"They obviously know exactly where they're going," laughed Maggie.

"I bet they take the same route every day. We used to have ducks on the farm at home and they always came home at the same time

every evening."

"It's a wonder they haven't been run over on this road," commented Maggie.

We were soon through the village and trotting along the narrow farm lane to Mary's house. Large flat fields lay on either side of us. Some were grass for cutting but others were showing bright green shoots of corn, shimmering in the afternoon sunshine.

"What a lovely old farmhouse," exclaimed Maggie. "Is that Mary's?"

"Yes. It has a timeless appearance, like it's been there for ever." We could see the Land Rover and trailer in the yard and as we approached, Mary's two dogs, a Labrador and a Springer Spaniel, barked a welcome at us. I slid down from the saddle as Mary came out of the house.

"Bring them into the big shed to untack them, then they can go in the calf paddock," she said. We followed on, leading the horses, as she led the way into the huge shed, which is more like a covered yard.

As we clattered over the cement passageway, a horse whinnied out.

"Have you got a horse again, Mary?" I asked curiously.

"No, I'm too old for that now," she laughed. "There are two horses here. They belong to my neighbours in the bungalow." We soon had the saddles and bridles off our horses and led them through where Mary had opened a large sliding door on the far side of the passageway.

"Oh, how smashing," Maggie exclaimed. "They'll love this." The calf paddock had once been an orchard. Old, gnarled fruit trees were still growing here and there and underneath a good growth of luscious, green grass covered the ground. Danny-boy and Cammy trotted out, heads tossing and after both had had a good roll in the long grass were soon chomping avidly at the tasty forage. We decided not to sheet them up until later as it was such a lovely afternoon and their saddle patches would dry out quicker in the fresh air. Allan had already taken the luggage in and volunteered to fill the water trough for the horses while Maggie and I went in with Mary for a drink of coffee.

After removing our boots, we went into the large lounge. A welcoming log fire blazed in the huge grate. It was bliss to sit and relax a while, knowing another day had been safely completed. Allan soon came and joined us and we all chatted and talked, discussing the events of the day. Then Mary announced that she was going into Northallerton and invited me to go along with her, adding,

"You can have a nice, quiet read at the paper, Allan. Put your feet up and relax."

"Aye, I'll do that. I might even fall asleep," he joked. I smiled across at Maggie, curled up on the settee, her cheeks rosy with the hot coffee and heat from the fire. It had been a tiring day for us and the horses.

"You can have all the time you want in the bath, Maggie," I told her.

"Mm, that sounds wonderful, if I can drag myself from this settee," she answered, smiling.

Five minutes later, Mary and I were speeding up the road towards Northallerton. As she drove, always as if it was an emergency, she told me about the evening she had planned. We were on our way to pick up meat pies ordered from the butcher's. She had organized a 'Pie and Pea' supper and disco at the pub in Maunby. Tickets had been selling well so Mary was hoping to make quite a bit of money for my funds. After collecting the pies, we made one or two more calls, including the local supermarket and were soon on our way back to the farm, delivering the pies on the way.

I knew this would be our only chance to have a chat. I guess that's why Mary invited me along. We talked about old school pals and our families, catching up on all the news, and in no time at all, we were turning up the farm lane.

"Maggie's a grand lass, isn't she?" said Mary.

"Yes. I was so pleased when I knew she was able to come with me. She's always such good fun and gets along with everyone." We pulled up outside the house and carried in the shopping.

"You go and get your bath now Ann and then we'll all have a drink," Mary suggested. Allan was sitting where we'd left him.

"Did you have a good rest, Al?" I asked him.

"Aye, I think I must have dozed off, it was so quiet. That'll soon change though, won't it?" he said, winking at me.

"What do you mean by that remark Mr. Bowes?" laughed Mary. "Anyway, where's Maggie?"

"She went to sheet Cammy up. Would you like me to see to Danny-Boy for you?" asked Allan.

"Yes please. That would be great, and then I can go straight upstairs. See you all later."

I hadn't realized how tired I was and I must have fallen asleep in the bath for when I looked at my watch, it was almost seven o'clock. When I went downstairs, I found Maggie laying the table.

"I thought we were having supper out?" I queried.

"Well, Mary's cooking dinner," said Maggie. I went to find her.

"You shouldn't have gone to all that trouble, Mary."

"You need to keep your stamina up," she replied. "Anyway, it's no trouble," she added, beaming at me.

"Lets have that drink then. I'll go and bring our sherry in."

"Now that's a good idea," she said. I returned with the still half-full bottle from the Land Rover.

"You'll find some glasses in the sideboard. Get the wine glasses out while you're at it," Mary shouted from the kitchen. Allan poured us all a drink as Mary came in with some juicy slices of melon.

"Help yourselves to these. Dinner's almost ready."

"Thank you Mary, those look good," declared Maggie, dragging her gaze away from the window. "That is an amazing view, isn't it?"

We all turned and looked through the window. Acres of flat, rich, farmland stretched away before us. Trees and hedges divided the patchwork of different greens. In the far distance, highlighted by the evening sunlight, we could see the steep, wooded hillsides below the impressive Whitestone cliff.

"Yes, it's very clear tonight. Tomorrow we'll be riding up there, Maggie."

"Do you know, I'm beginning to believe we might just manage this ride," she said.

"Of course you'll do it," Mary declared, bringing in the dinner.

Soon we were all tucking into roast leg of lamb, with jacket potatoes and loads of lovely fresh vegetables. A bottle of wine, which Maggie provided, complemented our food and we laughed and talked while enjoying our meal. It was good to sit and relax later in comfy chairs after hours riding in the saddle, as we drank our coffee round the crackling log fire. All too soon it was time to move. Maggie and I helped with the dishes, while Al went to get washed and changed. Shortly after, we were in Mary's car returning to the pub in Maunby.

The place was nearly full and we were lucky to find a free table. I couldn't possibly eat any more but Mary insisted that Allan have his pie and peas. We all managed a few drinks and Maggie and I had to answer a lot of questions about our ride. People wanted to know where we'd ridden from, what the rest of our route would be and how long it would take us. They showed a lot of interest in our fund-raising and asked about other things we were doing along the way. I felt a little in awe at the interest we were creating.

Later, Mary insisted that we should get up and dance, saying people would expect it. Maggie didn't take much persuading. After a few Jack Daniels, she would have danced all night! Everyone made us very welcome and I tried to thank as many people as possible for coming along and supporting us.

It was good to be back at Mary's, for I was more than ready for my bed.

"Anyone having a nightcap?" Mary asked cheerfully. "I'm having a brandy." As she had been driving, she hadn't been drinking since our wine over dinner.

"Not for me, thanks," said Maggie, looking tired.

"Me neither," I replied. "I'm sure Al will enjoy a drink with you though. I'm for bed," I smiled at them both. "Thanks for everything Mary. You're a star." I turned and followed Maggie up the stairs.

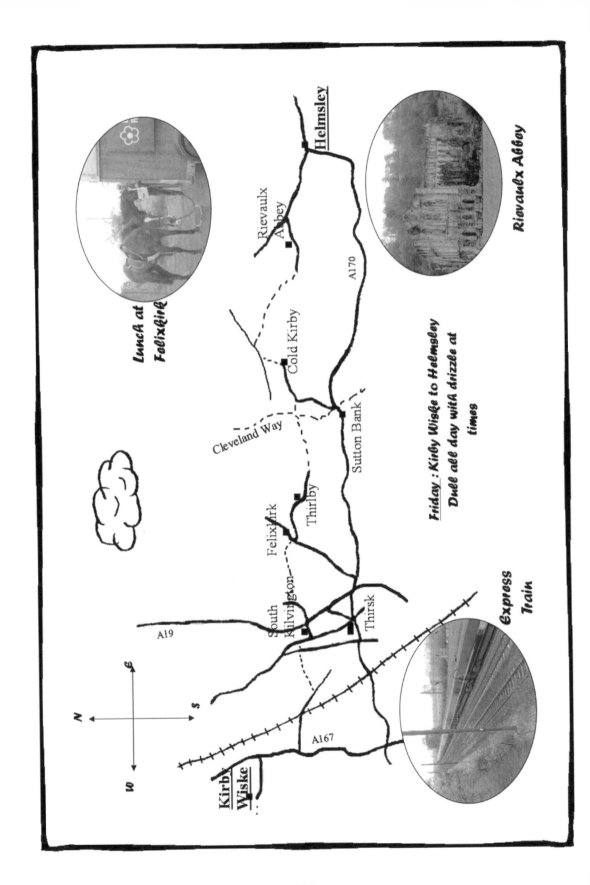

Lunch at Felixkirk

Rievaulx Abbey

Express Train

Friday : Kirby Wiske to Helmsley
Dull all day with drizzle at times

Helmsley

Rievaulx Abbey

A170

Cold Kirby

Cleveland Way

Sutton Bank

Thirlby

Felixkirk

South Kilvington

Thirsk

A19

A167

Kirby Wiske

N

W

E

S

FRIDAY MAY 26
KIRBY WISKE TO
HELMSLEY

"Maggie, Maggie!"

I had got up just before seven and, on entering the lounge, found Maggie curled up on the settee, fully dressed in her riding gear. Panic swept through me. Was she all right? Had something happened? I hadn't heard anything during the night. I stood over her still form, repeating her name softly. Suddenly, to my relief, her eyes opened and a smile spread slowly across her face.

"Are you okay?" I asked anxiously.

"Yes, I'm fine." Slowly she sat up, rubbing her eyes. "You'll never guess what I did." Stretching her arms high above her head, she continued, "I set my alarm last night for seven o'clock and when it went off, I jumped out of bed in a hurry. When I came in here I saw that clock up there on the wall saying five past six!" She laughed as she told me her mistake. "It wasn't worth going back to bed so I just curled up on here."

"You had me worried. I thought something must have happened." I relaxed and smiled. "Come on, let's go and bring the horses in."

We were busy preparing the horses' feed in the trailer when a voice spoke from outside.

"Hi, you two. How are you this morning?" Mary had just returned from exercising her dogs across the fields.

"Fine thanks," I replied. "Maggie gave me a bit of a fright, though." Mary laughed,

"I saw her there, sleeping soundly," she said, grinning up at Maggie. "You looked all right, Maggie, so I left you in peace."

"I felt a right fool when I saw the time. I must have been half asleep when I set my alarm, I think," she added, stepping down from the trailer. We made our way to the large shed as Mary fastened up the dogs.

"I'll go and be getting breakfast ready, while you're seeing to the horses," she called after us. We received a loud welcome from the resident horses when they heard our voices and Danny-Boy and Cammy instantly responded.

"They sound happy enough, anyway," said Maggie, as we pushed open the large sliding door to the orchard. We soon had them both in and tethered to the partition in the passageway, where we gave them their hand food. After grooming and examining them we left them in peace to finish their rations.

Back in the house, we found Allan tucking into a large breakfast of bacon and egg.

"What about you girls?" asked Mary, "would you like the same?"

"No thanks," answered Maggie. "I'll just have cereal, if that's okay."

"Me neither, Mary, but may I have a bacon butty please," I asked.

"Sure. No problem," she replied. "Help yourselves to a cup of tea and fill your flasks Ann, ready for your lunch. You can make some sandwiches after breakfast, too, to take with you."

"Great, thanks Mary. Maggie and I can do that while Al's loading up the luggage once more."

After breakfast, with all our bags packed yet again, it was time to tack up the horses and be on our way. Maggie and I led the horses round to the front of the house. We each gave Mary a big thank you hug before mounting up. Danny-Boy was impatient to be off, maybe sensing that we were getting nearer to home. He tossed his head when I let him go and set off at a lively pace down the farm lane towards Kirby Wiske. It was just gone nine o'clock and Helmsley seemed a long way away. Still, at least it was dry this morning.

Allan caught up with us in the village, saying that he would wait near the main road. He thought it best if he followed closely behind us for the short distance we had to travel on the busy Northallerton road. The traffic is quite heavy at this time of morning and there is little or no grass verge for us to ride on. We trotted briskly along this section and were relieved to arrive at the whitewashed cottage without mishap, where we took the left turn. Allan went on ahead to meet up with Mary, where they would wait for us.

Five minutes later we were approaching the bridge over the main North – South railway line. I had almost reached the centre of the bridge when my worst fears were realized. I heard the roar of an express train approaching. Rather than risk panicking Danny-Boy by rushing to get off the bridge, I halted him and forced myself to relax. I patted his neck and spoke quietly to him as the train thundered it's way below us. I could feel Danny-Boy tremble beneath me as the bridge vibrated but he never moved a foot. Maybe he was too petrified. As the sound of that mechanical monster faded in the distance, I eased the reins and walked him quietly off the bridge.

"That was a bit scary, wasn't it?" Maggie came trotting up along side me. "I was about twenty yards behind you when I heard the train, so I waited until it had passed."

"Yeah, I didn't know how Danny-Boy would react. It all happened so quickly; I don't think he had time to panic. I was very pleased with him all the same." We were trotting on a quiet country road in open farmland and it wasn't long before we saw the Land Rover parked up ahead at Woodhill Grange. Mary was there too. They were waiting by the roadside opposite the farmhouse. This was where we were to leave the road and take the bridleway to South Kilvington. We had to say goodbye to Mary here as she was now going back home.

"Good luck lasses with the rest of the ride. I'll ring you, Ann, when I know the final total of money raised last night."

"Okay, and thanks again for everything Mary. You will come over, won't you?"

"Yes, I hope so. So long then." We set off through the farmyard, turning to wave as we closed the gate behind us.

"I really hope she does come to see you," said Maggie, as we trotted down the broad cart track at the side of the field. "I'd love to see her again. She's such a super person."

"Me too. She's been a great friend to me, always ready to help when asked."

We continued on in amicable silence, each with our own thoughts of Mary and all she had done for us. Birds were whistling and singing in the hedgerows and a tractor could be heard droning away in the distance. All the fields were flat and very large compared to fields back home. As the sound of the machinery drew closer, we were able to look over the hedgerow alongside the next field and could see a huge tractor working.

"Wow, I'll have to take a picture of that for Lewis, he'll just love it," exclaimed Maggie. Lewis is her youngest son and tractor mad. I stood and watched the huge tractor pulling the most enormous crop sprayer I'd ever seen

"You'd never get that *into* our fields," I commented. Maggie finished taking her pictures and we carried on, passing a large plantation on our right. As we neared the end of the trees, we could see the village of South Kilvington two fields farther on. The bridleway ended at the road, which we crossed, and we found the small handgate leading into a pasture on the other side.

"Where now?" asked Maggie.

"Down there, over that foot bridge," I replied, pointing ahead of us. We walked towards the bridge over the stream.

"Not very wide, is it?" remarked Maggie as we approached it.

"No, but at least it looks strong. Go on, take Cammy over. She's been over narrower ones." Looking a little wary Maggie urged Cammy on to the bridge. She very calmly walked over and without too much hesitation, Danny-Boy followed, his shoes clattering on the wooden planks.

"We have another stream to cross now, over there past that huge oak tree."

"Gosh, it is big isn't it?" remarked Maggie, as we rode underneath its enormous umbrella of leafy branches. There was a tall hedge bordering the stream and a gate that we had to open, leading down into the water.

"Looks like a getting off job," I said slipping down from my saddle. It was very wet and muddy and the gate needed lifting. I nearly got stuck in the mud.

"Never mind," said Maggie laughing, "at least you can wash your boots off in the water." When Maggie and Cammy had squelched through the mud into the stream, I closed the gate. I cleaned my boots in the water as Maggie had suggested before climbing back in the saddle. We gave the horses the opportunity to have a drink before riding out of the water on to the hard surface on the other side. There was a large, tall, house standing by the stream.

"Looks like an old water-mill, doesn't it," I suggested.

"Mm, I think you're right," Maggie replied. "It's made a big home for someone, hasn't it?" Once in the main street, we turned right, through the village, passing by the old church and graveyard with its ancient yew trees. It is a quiet, sprawling village with lots of trees and well-kept gardens. We turned left on to the road to Upsall, where several gardens had Cherry trees, radiant in full blossom. We could hear the continuous rumble of vehicles as we neared the busy A19. The horses seemed oblivious to the roar as we rode underneath the bridge that carried a never-ending stream of traffic.

With the deafening noise still in our ears, we turned right up a lane signposted Manor Farm. Dandelions and stitchwort adorned the sides of the lane and the occasional crop of bright, yellow, oilseed rape filled the air with its sickly pungent smell. We continued along this quiet farm lane for over a mile, until we reached Hagg House Farm. Here free-range hens busied themselves under the hedgerows and scratched about in the dusty soil. There were all different colours, including black, brown, white and old-fashioned speckled ones.

The road ended here in the farmyard and we continued on a bridleway across the fields towards Felixkirk. We could see the village, quite a way ahead of us, and also the distinguishing white-stone cliffs in the distance that still seemed a long way off.

Sheep with their lambs were contentedly grazing, some of which were on creep feed and we rode quietly through without disturbing them too much. To our left rose wooded hills stretching north to Osmotherly. It was peaceful and quiet away from the traffic with just the singing of the birds in the hedgerows and the occasional bleating of a sheep calling to her young lambs. It was warm and still with no breeze.

We had ridden to within two fields off Felixkirk, when our track

came to an abrupt end with only a single track going off to the left.

"Where now?" queried Maggie.

"Don't know. It's no good going along that way." I indicated the track to our left. There had been a huge trench dug along the edge of the field to our right but we couldn't see a track anywhere.

"Look," exclaimed Maggie. "There's a girl riding towards us down this other track. She's sure to know the way." We waited until the rider drew near and then asked her for some guidance.

"You have to detour round that huge trench, then you'll find a track up the side of that next field," she informed us with a smile. "It's a bit misleading if you're not familiar with the area because they've dug up the bridleway."

"Thanks very much. It's a good job you came along when you did," I told her. We chatted a while longer, explaining what we were doing, then set off. Soon we were trotting up a grassy field alongside a thick hawthorn hedge to a gate at the top, where Allan was waiting. He opened the gate for us, saying,

"You've made good time. It's only quarter past eleven. The horses look warm."

"Yes, it's quite sticky. They'll be ready for a drink," replied Maggie. Allan had managed to find a small parking area on the edge of the village. We tied the horses to the back of the trailer and poured water into their buckets for them. While they drank, Maggie and I removed our jackets then loosened the girths on the saddles to let the horses' backs cool off. After giving Danny-Boy a small ration of hand food, I sat down on the grass with some railings for a backrest. I had a long drink of orange juice before eating my sandwiches.

Maggie sponged Cammy's neck down with cold water before coming to join me. The heavy scent of May blossom drifted across from the hedgerow. We could hear bees at work as they went about their frantic task of collecting pollen and now and then the repetitive clicking of a grasshopper added to the chorus of birdsong. Had I closed my eyes, it would have been easy to drift off to sleep but we hadn't time for that. We were due to meet up with Desert Orchid and his rider, Sue at two o'clock and had a fair distance to ride before then.

Lunch over, we helped Allan side everything up and pack bowls and buckets back in the Land Rover. Although the weather had clouded over, we didn't bother with our waterproofs, as we knew it would be warm work climbing out through the wood. Having tightened our girths we were soon back in the saddle and on the road to Thirlby, leaving behind the quiet little village of Felixkirk.

It was a very narrow country lane bordered by tall hedgerows or fences. Stitchwort, ragged robin and bluebells abounded in the grass verges. It was as well that there was little traffic, as passing places were few and far between. We met the milk tanker but were fortunate enough to be near a gateway, so avoided any mishap. Soon we had completed the mile and a half into the sleepy village of Thirlby. It was full of neat, picturesque cottages and well-kept gardens. Many shrubs were out and the scent of lilac blossom filled the air.

At the far end of the village, we walked through a ford, letting the horses cool their feet. Once through the village, we found ourselves climbing steadily until at last the sheer rock face of the Whitestone Cliffs came into view above the trees.

"Wow! That looks rather daunting," exclaimed Maggie, as we trotted along the last stretch of road to the cottage at the foot of the hillside.

"Yes, it seems much more severe when you get this close. I hope the bridleway doesn't go that way."

"Don't you know what the track's like?" asked Maggie.

"No. Allan and I just came as far as this cottage." We had reached the end of the hard road and started up the track leading into the trees.

Not very far in, the track divided.

"Which way now?"

"I'm not sure," I replied. "We'll try this way." We took the right-handed route but it soon turned even more to the right.

"This can't be right," said Maggie.

"No, we need to be heading up the hill more. Let's try the other one." We turned and retraced our tracks, this time taking the steep, left-handed track. The bridleway was very narrow with the trees forming a canopy of green over our heads. It was wet and boggy in places so we had to climb up on to the bank at the sides of the track and find a way between the trees, avoiding the low branches. In some of the wetter places clumps of golden marsh marigolds were growing. The curled, pale green fronds of the bracken were just emerging and bluebells and forget-me-nots abounded. Here and there were patches of the shy, graceful wood anemones.

Birds were calling and singing all around us and now and then we heard a shriek from an alarmed pheasant. I kept urging Danny-Boy up the rugged track, always heading higher and often slanting out to the left, as it was too severe to climb straight up. I looked back every now and then but Cammy was doing fine, following on close behind us. After twenty minutes, we stopped to let the horses have a breather. Eventually we reached the summit, where our track joined the Cleveland Way. Leaving the trees behind, we found ourselves on what seemed like the top of the world. It was raining lightly, which we hadn't noticed while we'd made our way up the track beneath the trees. Looking around, we could see for miles.

"What a fantastic view," murmured Maggie in awe, gazing across the vista of verdant countryside stretched out before us.

"That's amazing, isn't it? It's a pity it's not clearer."

"I'm still going to take a picture," declared Maggie.

We struck off on the bridleway pointing to Dialstone Farm, up the side of a large field. It was much cooler up here and the trees grew stunted and bent from the harsh winter weather. Beyond the limestone wall on our right grew clumps of bilberry and heather, not seen since we were on the Pennines. As we drew closer to the farm, we noticed a large, flat green field on our right with a worn track round the outside.

"Must be the training gallops for the racing stables," I said.

"Mm, there are some stables over at Hambleton. It's amazing how flat it is, isn't it?"

"Yeay," I agreed. "I bet there are some cold days when riding up here in winter."

"It's a bit bleak, isn't it?" Suddenly she pointed, "Look, there's

Allan, over there on the road." By now we had almost reached the farm.

"I think we'd better get our waterproofs off him." The rain was just a drizzle but the skies looked dull and grey. Allan asked us about our climb up the hillside, as we prepared ourselves for the rain. We were soon ready and back in the saddle and set off at a trot down the road towards Cold Kirby.

"I'll wait by the forestry gate," Allan shouted through his window as he drove past us.

We by-passed the aptly named village of Cold Kirby and continued on the road to Old Byland. Soon we arrived where Allan was waiting by the entrance to the forest ride.

"I'll see you later. I hope you make it on time," he said, as I turned to close the forestry gate behind us.

"Yeay." I smiled and waved before setting off alongside Maggie, down the rough forestry road. I didn't know at the time how far it was to the other end but I knew that we were going to have to keep a steady pace to be at our rendezvous with Dessie on time. Richard Burridge had again come to my aid and had agreed that Dessie could ride into Helmsley with us, as a publicity stunt, to draw the crowds. I was hoping for a good collection, as I had widely advertised his arrival and it was market day.

We were descending slowly as we made our way through the forestry. Round each bend I hoped to see the exit gate but always there was more road. The rain had almost ceased and it was humid and sticky among the trees. Eventually we reached the valley bottom where a stream flowed into a small lake. Some ducks flew off the water as we trotted by.

"It's beautiful down here, isn't it?" commented Maggie.

"Yes, very peaceful. I just wish we weren't having to rush so much."

"What time do we meet up with Dessie?"

"Two o'clock and it's half past one now." We kept urging the horses on, not daring to stop for a walk and, thankfully, the exit gate appeared round the next bend. Back on the tarmac road once more, the horses found it easier going and we pushed on through the few dwellings by the bridge over the stream. We caught a glimpse of the wonderful old ruins of Rievaulx Abbey through the trees, but hadn't time to stop and admire it.

"How much further, is it?" asked Maggie as we began climbing the bank out of the valley.

"Two miles," I replied. "I wish I hadn't put these waterproofs back on. I'm about boiling."

"Me too. I can feel my shirt sticking to my back. I bet I look like a beetroot." The horses were finding it hard work as we urged them on up the steep hillside. The scent of bluebells drifted in the air and looking up to my left, I saw the bank side under the trees awash with a sea of blue. Eventually we reached the top of the bank and after a further ten minutes, saw the large horsebox parked in a field entrance, a hundred yards ahead of us. We'd just made it. It was five minutes to two.

It wasn't just the horses that arrived tired, hot and sweaty, to be greeted by Sue, already mounted on Dessie. He was looking superb and very sure of himself. As we chatted to Sue and Allan, who was also parked at the roadside, Maggie and I dismounted and began to strip off once more. Danny-Boy and Cammy stood patiently waiting, not bothering to move, as Maggie and I sorted ourselves out and handed Allan all our discarded belongings.

At last we were ready to ride the two miles into Helmsley. Richard suggested that Dessie ride with us this short distance to settle him down, hoping he would then stand nice and quiet for his admirers. As we approached the town, I thought it would be nice if Dessie rode between Danny-Boy and Cammy but every time Sue tried to come between us, Danny-Boy edged over and refused to let him get anywhere near Cammy. We laughed about his protectiveness and let him have his way until we neared the town. I think by then he had reluctantly accepted the presence of Dessie.

We rode into the market place to a rousing welcome. There were throngs of people who cheered and clapped their hands. I began to recognise people I knew - it was lovely to see familiar faces after all those miles and miles of riding. Chris was there with the three children, who couldn't contain their excitement at seeing their Mum again. Joe was there too, with a loud-hailer informing the crowds about Dessie's arrival. Dawne's daughter, Annabel, and her Gran were putting on tabards and starting out with the collecting boxes. Lots of people were taking photographs and there was a photographer from the local *Gazette* wanting Dessie to pose for pictures.

It was great to see so many people there, even though it was raining yet again. Danny-Boy wasn't very impressed with the umbrellas that were going up all around him. I don't think he'd ever seen one before. I know most of the crowd were there to see Dessie but I like to think that some were there to congratulate Maggie and me on getting this

far. So many people were there, stroking the horses and asking about the ride, that I hardly noticed the rain. It felt so good to be back among our own people and I now really believed, for the first time, that we would complete this ride.

There were people working in the shops who wanted Dessie to walk round the market square so they could see him. Sue agreed, so we all set off but Dessie was a little nervous of the market stalls and wares everywhere, as there wasn't much room to ride between them. I asked Danny-Boy to go forward and he carefully made his way between all the cars and stalls, with Dessie and Cammy following along behind. He may not be famous but I was very proud of him. Once back on the street, I let Dessie come to the front again where the press were waiting to photograph him. How he loves the cameras! He has such a wonderful head carriage and proud expression in his eyes.

All too soon the allotted time for Dessie to stay with us had run out, so we had to make our farewells. Allan was busy gathering in all the collecting boxes. It later proved to have been a very successful day financially. Having said goodbye to Sue and Dessie, Maggie and I made our way down the road and round to Dawne's field on the edge of town. Annabel was there waiting for us and, while we were busy untacking the horses in a small enclosure adjoining the field, she explained the arrangements that she'd made for the following morning. She had to go to work, so was going to bring the horses in early and tether them inside the enclosure to feed them. We made up their feed in bowls and Annabel took these home with her. Having sheeted up the horses, we turned them loose in the field. They promptly galloped off down to the hedge at the bottom to make friends with the other horses. I wondered if Ruby recognized her son as they nickered softly to each other. I like to think that she did.

"Well, that's another day over." Maggie was leaning on the fence next to me as we watched our horses.

"Yes, only two to go. It was hard work today, wasn't it?"

"Mm, I'll sleep tonight, if my kids will let me. It was lovely to see them again." She sighed. "I've never been away from them for that long before."

"Don't you two want to go home today?" Chris had pulled up in his vehicle with all the children. Home! It had a nice ring to it.

"Yes, we're ready. I've just got my tack to load up," Maggie answered, smiling up at them all.

"See you in the morning, Maggie," I called after her. They were all waving as I made my way to the Land Rover with my saddle and bridle, where Allan was waiting to take me home. Seemed odd going home without Danny-Boy. We were soon crossing the all too familiar moors back into Fryup Dale. I don't think it had ever looked so beautiful. I couldn't believe how many miles we'd ridden. Was it only Sunday that we'd left?

There was plenty to do when we arrived home. After unloading all our luggage, I set about making some tea while Allan went to feed the dogs. Tony and Stella had left the previous day. They were due to meet their son's future in-laws that weekend, so needed an early start. Sara had been over in the morning to exercise the dogs after taking the children to school. They would be arriving back at six o'clock as usual, to stay overnight with us while Sara went to work.

The house was very clean and tidy, with all the laundry neatly washed and ironed in piles in the bedrooms. Good old Stella, she's a great lass. Might be a good idea to go away more often! Allan and I were just having our drink of tea after our meal when the phone rang. It was Mick.

"You've got back all right then?" he asked.

"Yes thanks. How are you feeling?"

"Oh, just same as usual. I'll have to go to bed soon. We haven't been back from hospital long. I was wondering about tomorrow."

"Are you still hoping to ride with us?"

"Aye, for part 'et way, anyway. I've another rider going along with us to help me out."

"Sara's coming to ride on Cloey, so we can pick Velvet up on our way over. We left Danny-Boy and Cammy at Dawne's."

"That'll do then. What time?"

"Eight thirty at your lane-end but the Land Rover will be full as all the bairns are coming."

"That's all right. Joyce will bring me over in the car. I'm off to bed now. Don't feel too good. See you tomorrow."

"Okay. Bye Mick." He would have received another massive dose of chemo' that day. I don't know where he gets his courage to even think about riding. His horse, Velvet, is a beautiful black thoroughbred, standing at 16. 1.hands. Mick bought her as a four year old and she stayed with me for several weeks. She was very green and I took her out on the moors with Danny-Boy, so they are very good mates. She also came to me the following year and I did some elementary jumping with her. She is a lovely smooth ride but with immense power.

Shortly after I came off the phone, Sara arrived with the children. I told her what time we would be leaving in the morning, then she dashed off to work. It was lovely to see the children and they were very excited about going along with Grandad the next day. I settled them down to watch their favourite cartoon, while I took our cases upstairs and unpacked. Allan went to sort out the trailer, which had to be emptied to make room for Velvet and Cloey. The Land Rover, too, needed tidying up, as the children would be travelling in the back.

By the time I'd finished upstairs and done the washing up, it was time to get the children their supper and ready for bed. I didn't have any trouble getting them off, as they knew we had to be up early the next morning.

"What time are we setting off, Nan?" asked Adam as I tucked him and Jimmy into bed

"Oh, just before eight o'clock."

"Will Mum be here?" Jimmy asked.

"I hope so. She's going to ride Cloey," I replied as I kissed them goodnight. Josie got an extra cuddle when I tucked her in.

"Did you have a good birthday?"

"Yes. Mum made me a cake with candles on"

"And how old are you now?"

"Five."

"Wow, that's ever so old. Off to sleep now. See you in the morning, sweetie."

"Night, Nan."

"Night, night." When I went downstairs, Allan had just come in.

"All in bed?" he asked.

"Yes."

"Won't be long before I'm off, too. Are you bringing Cloey in?"

"Yes. I think I'd better. The forecast's not too good." I went out to the stable and put some food in the feeder, then went down to the bottom field and called Cloey who was under the hill out of sight. She soon came trotting up the field when she heard my voice. I let her through the hand gate and she followed me back to the stable. She nuzzled my face as I stroked her, as if to say she was pleased we were back. She looked fine and all her shoes were intact. I returned to the house and gratefully sank into a comfy chair, accepting the drink Allan had poured for me.

"Thanks. It's good to be home, isn't it?"

"Aye, it is."

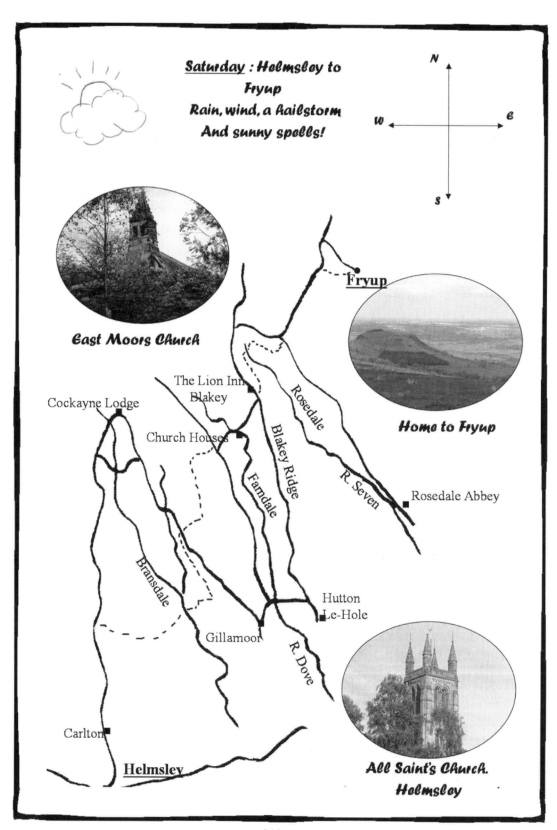

Saturday : Helmsley to
Fryup
Rain, wind, a hailstorm
And sunny spells!

East Moors Church

Fryup

Home to Fryup

The Lion Inn
Blakey

Cockayne Lodge

Church Houses

Rosedale

Blakey Ridge

Farndale

R. Seven

Rosedale Abbey

Bransdale

Hutton
Le-Hole

Gillamoor

R. Dove

Carlton

Helmsley

All Saint's Church.
Helmsley

SATURDAY MAY 27
HELMSLEY TO
FRYUP

I awoke to the sound of rain lashing against the window. Back home, in the comfort of my own bed, it took me a moment to recall what day it was. Realisation dawned. It was Saturday, and I was still riding. I dressed hurriedly and went downstairs to find the children up and watching television.

"Hello Nan," from Josie.

"Hi, you're all up early. Where's Grandad?"

"He's gone out to do the dogs," Adam informed me. "I didn't want to go with him this morning." Normally he goes everywhere with Grandad.

"Don't blame you in this weather," I said, as I set about getting them their breakfast. With them all tucking into their cereal, I put the kettle on before dashing out with a coat pulled over my head to give Cloey a feed. She nickered softly to me as I entered the stable.

"Good job I brought you in last night, wasn't it miss?" I patted her soft, silky neck as she munched her food. She wouldn't take much grooming. When I returned to the house, Sara had just arrived.

"What a morning, Mam."

"Yes, isn't it. I bet you wish you weren't coming now," I said.

" No, I'm looking forward to it," she replied cheerfully.

"I hope you've got some waterproofs."

"I've got my coat but haven't any leggings."

"Never mind, I'm sure Dad will have a pair you can borrow." I was hastily getting my breakfast when Allan came back in, shaking the water from his cap.

"It's ever so wet out there. I hope it eases up a bit for you."

"Me too. Would you like a flask making?"

"Good idea. Yes please," he replied.

"I'll pack some chocolate snacks for the bairns as well."

After breakfast, Sara washed up and got the children ready for their trip out, while I went to tack up Cloey and load her into the trailer. The children were very excited about going in the Land Rover with Grandad to see Nan and Mummy go on the 'Big Ride'. By eight o'clock, we had everything loaded. Thankfully, there was more room now and the children were quite happy in the back of the Land Rover with Danny-Boy's saddle and bridle. Sara and I squashed in the front with Allan, all togged up in our waterproofs with hats, crops, and collecting boxes and tabards for the collectors. We set off up the road across the moors to Hutton-le-Hole, where we were picking up Velvet.

As we approached the road end leading up to Mick's farm, we could see Mick standing by his car, holding Velvet by the lead rein. I could see that she was already tacked up under her sheet. Her bridle was on too, under the headcollar. I quickly jumped out and took Velvet from him, so that he could get back in the car with Joyce, his wife, out of the rain. I noticed the young girl, Joanne, whom Mick had spoken of, in the car with Joyce. Allan had opened the trailer door and I led Velvet up the ramp alongside Cloey.

"We'll follow along after you," shouted Mick through the car window as I climbed back into the Land Rover. We continued on our way to Helmsley.

As we pulled up alongside Dawne's field, we could see Danny-Boy and Cammy tethered to the fence inside the enclosure, as promised by Annabelle, their feed bowls now empty. There was a great deal of welcoming neighing from all the horses as we unloaded Velvet and Cloey. I was removing Danny-Boy's sheet when Chris drew up with Maggie, who quickly set to, getting Cammy ready. Joanne, the girl Mick had enrolled to help out, was riding the first stretch on Velvet. It wasn't long before all four of us were mounted up and ready for off.

Although it was still raining quite hard, the horses were full of high spirits, revelling in each other's company, as we set off up Carlton Road at a brisk pace. Sara and I turned and waved to the three smiling faces of the children watching us leave. Mick was travelling with Allan but Joyce was returning home and coming back later to meet up with us at lunchtime.

We soon left Helmsley behind as we trotted between green hedgerows with large arable fields on either side. We made our way up the gradual climb and passed through the tiny village of Carlton. The occasional clump of trees gave us some shelter from the rain as we continued on the road to Newgate Foot. From here, as we descended the bank into the valley, we could see the vast expanse of moorland in the distance. It was a little warmer in the valley bottom and we didn't notice the rain so much. We passed by one of the smallest churches in England at East Moors, its spire rising above the trees and rhododendron bushes. There were woods and areas of forestry on either side as we started to climb back up, leaving the valley behind.

At last, having ridden about six miles, we reached the open moor and in the distance, waiting by the roadside, we could see the familiar red banners on the Land Rover. There was quite a breeze blowing and the air was much cooler but the rain had eased considerably. Mick was standing by the vehicle, collar turned up and shoulders hunched against the cold wind. He was going to ride on Velvet across Bransdale with us.

"How's it going, lasses?"

"Okay, Velvet's settled down a bit now," I replied, as Joanne dismounted and held the reins for Mick.

"It's not too warm up here, is it?" he commented, as he struggled to climb on to Velvet. Since contracting leukaemia, Mick had problems with his circulation and often had difficulty keeping warm.

"It's not so bad when you're riding," said Maggie encouragingly.

"Good. Let's be off then." He gathered up his reins and led us down the rough track over the moor high above Bonfield Gill, towards the valley of Bransdale. It was great to be back on the moors with the wind in my face and hearing again all the familiar bird-calls. The curlews and grouse and the occasional golden plover were all wary of our intrusive presence, as they tended their newly hatched young.

The track started to bear left and suddenly, over the brow of the next heather-clad ridge, spread out before us, was the beautiful green valley of Bransdale. Farmsteads were visible, dotted among the patchwork of fields, which slope down the steep hillsides to the river below. On the far side of the valley we could see the large area of forestry where we would be riding. We descended slowly down the track towards the deserted dwelling of Stork Farm. Although there were sheep grazing with their lambs in the nearby fields, no-one had lived in the house for years.

As I jumped from my horse to take advantage of the privacy of the derelict buildings, I wondered who the last inhabitants had been in such a beautiful but isolated place. The roofs were caving in and there were only black, gaping holes where there used to be windows. It's sad to think that such places will never again be alive to the sound of children's laughter, no dogs barking a welcome or hens scratching around in the dusty soil.

"C'mon, are you going to take all day?" Maggie's voice floated through the open building. She was laughing as I emerged into the overgrown, neglected farmyard. I grinned back at her.

"You just want me to open the gate for you all." I led Danny-Boy to the small hand-gate and held it open while they all went through. In single file they set off down the narrow woodland track among the trees towards the beck. I was soon back in the saddle and caught up with them as we approached a very boggy area in the valley bottom near the stream.

"I'll go first, Mick, to open the gate. You can give them a lead over the beck." I circled round the worst of the bog and jumped off to open another small gate by the water's edge. I led Danny-Boy through and pulled him over on to a narrow piece of bankside between the fence and the water. There was quite a drop down into the beck. Mick followed close behind with Velvet and with only a little coaxing, she dropped down into the water and splashed her way over to the far bank. Maggie came next.

"Is it okay in the bottom?" she enquired warily as Velvet had stirred the water so it was now cloudy and muddy.

"Yes, it's fine. Cammy's been over before, anyway," I told her. Cammy didn't need much urging. She very carefully stepped off the camber into the water and followed Velvet on to the other side. Sara was still coaxing Cloey across the bog, and then had difficulty getting her through the gateway as Cloey could see the fast flowing stream.

"Lead her through and then I'll close the gate," I told Sara. She jumped off and with a bit of tugging, managed to get Cloey through on to the bank side. There wasn't a lot of room but she scrambled back into the saddle while I closed the gate.

"She'll never go through there," exclaimed Sara in awe.

"She'll have to. There's no other way," I told her. Mick and Maggie were shouting encouragement to her from the other side as she urged Cloey forward. Cloey had her front feet on the edge of the bank and wasn't quite sure how to go about this. Back in the saddle, I encouraged Cloey from behind with a gentle tap on the rump.

Suddenly, Cloey, in desperation, leaped into the water, hoping to reach the other side in one jump. As the stream was about fifteen feet across, this was impossible and she landed with an almighty splash in the middle of the stream. I don't know who screamed the loudest - Sara, because she only just made it back into the saddle from the air, or me, because I got pretty soaked as Cloey landed in the water, sending spray everywhere! With two more huge leaps, Cloey made it on to the opposite bank, to much cheering and laughter. Not wanting to be left behind, Danny-Boy plunged into the water and splashed his way across. I was still laughing and shaking the water from my clothes, when I reached the other side.

"Well done Sara! I wish I'd had that on the video." We were climbing up the muddy, stony track from the beck in single file to another hand-gate.

"I thought for a moment that I was going to end up in the water," she replied, laughing. Mick was opening the gate ahead of us.

"We'll close it, Mick. You go on ahead," I called to them. Through the gate was a large grass field stretching up the hillside to the forestry plantation. Mick set off at a canter up the field with Cammy in hot pursuit. Sara waited while I fastened the gate then we, too, let Danny-Boy and Cloey have their heads as we followed the others up the field. Cloey dropped her back and raced ahead of me, loving the challenge. We caught them up at the gate, leading into the forestry.

"That was good," exclaimed Sara breathlessly. "I think Cloey enjoyed it, too."

"More than her experience in the beck, I should think," I replied, still amused by the incident.

Once through the gate, we trotted the horses up the grassy forest ride. We had to walk them every now and then, where the going became very soft and boggy. After about ten minutes, we left the ride and turned right up a single-file track, slanting up the steep bank side between the trees. The horses had to pick their way over the stones and boggy patches and we had to avoid the occasional hanging branches. At one point, a fallen tree lay across our path and we had to detour round it, finding a way between the trees.

Eventually we came out on to a wide forest ride where we turned left-handed. The rain had almost ceased and the air was much cooler with a fresh breeze blowing. There were more fallen trees and branches across the ride and we had to wind our way round them as best we could. After a while, we reached a small gate, beyond which, was a belt of densely growing evergreens with only a narrow path for us to follow. Along here we had to keep a short distance between each rider to prevent getting a nasty backlash from the branches as we pushed our way through. It was a good job we had waterproofs on as the branches were hanging in water and showered us with water as we brushed through.

At last we emerged at the far end into a more open, shrubby area where the wind was blowing quite strongly away from the protection of the trees. We found ourselves high up on the east side of the valley and the view up the dale was quite spectacular. There were a few sheep with their lambs that scattered away in alarm, as we rode through, obviously not used to seeing many horse-riders. We were on a high ridge overlooking the valley with a steep wooded slope below us. The wind was blowing so strongly through the trees that we had to shout at each other to make ourselves heard.

Presently, we reached a gate leading on to the open moor and there, on the road half a mile away, was Allan's Land Rover. Maggie jumped off Cammy to open the gate, as it needed lifting. When she was back in the saddle, we all cantered along the rough rutted track, avoiding the potholes and clumps of seves, over the moor to the road. It was exhilarating to feel the wind in my face and sense the excitement in the horses as we raced towards the road. The children greeted us with smiling faces, hoods pulled over their heads to keep out the cold.

"Right, Joanne you can have another go." Mick looked pale as he slid wearily from the saddle and handed the reins to her.

"Are you okay?" I asked anxiously. He smiled.

"Aye. I will be after a bit when I get in't Land Rover and have a drink of Al's coffee. You lasses get going over that moor." Joanne was now mounted on Velvet once more and ready for off, so I turned Danny-Boy up the moor in the direction of Farndale. As the others followed, Allan called after me and I turned in my saddle.

"We'll see you at bottom o' Blakey Bank."

"Right. Bye." I waved, and then concentrated on where we were going. When we had climbed out on to the top of the moor, our track joined the well-marked route known as the old Stokesley road. It runs the full length of Rudland Rigg and is very popular with walkers. It was good travelling for the horses and we chatted to each other as we trotted along together, enjoying the freedom of the wild beauty all around us.

A mile or more further on, we branched off on a bridleway that would eventually take us down into Farndale. We often had to resort to walking, as this track was rough with lots of loose stones and pebbles. On the distant skyline we could see the outline of the Lion Inn at Blakey, our lunchtime venue.

"It looks a long way off yet," said Sara, as I was pointing it out to them. None of the other girls had ever been up here before.

"I bet it's rough up here in the winter," remarked Maggie. "It's bad enough today."

"Could be worse. It could be snowing!" I joked. It certainly felt cold enough for snow. Gradually our track started to descend and we picked our way carefully down the steep bank side. The broad expanse of the dale spread out before us. Down in the valley bottom, we could see the small cluster of dwellings known as Church Houses. Small fronds of bracken were beginning to unfurl on the craggy bank sides and the tough moor sheep were nibbling the short sparse grass trying to grow there. Eventually we arrived at the gate leading into the fields. We had only one field to ride down before reaching the hard road where we turned right and trotted on to the junction at Monket Bank. This bit of road, leading down to the valley bottom, is very steep and narrow, so I hoped we wouldn't meet much traffic. As we neared the bridge over the stream, we noticed the last of the famous Farndale daffodils still in bloom along by the river.

We trotted on to Church Houses and as there was no sign of the Land Rover we let the horses walk leisurely on to the junction at the bottom of Blakey bank, passing the show field and the small, secluded church by the stream. It was much warmer down here in the valley, away from the harsh winds of the moors. We had to wait a short while for Allan but it gave the horses a rest before climbing up the steep hillside to Blakey Ridge.

I think Joanne was glad when Mick said that he would ride Velvet up the bank. I don't think she was used to such distances and was glad of a ride in the Land Rover. With Mick safely in the saddle, we set off up the hill.

"Have you been waiting long?" he asked.

"Only five or ten minutes," Maggie replied.

"Well, you can't 'ave wasted much time coming ovver't moor."

"You had a lot further to travel than us. It's miles round by Gillamoor, especially with a Land Rover and trailer," I said. Cammy was trotting full speed ahead of us all, up the bank.

"She must have smelled home, Maggie," I called to her. Maggie's home in Rosedale was just over the ridge top. Maggie laughed.

"She's going to get a shock, isn't she?" was her reply. Looking back, I noticed that Cloey was lagging behind, struggling to keep up with us. I waited for her to catch up.

"Nearly there, Sara, then Cloey will get rested up while we have lunch." We were nearing the top of the bank where it was noticeably cooler. As we arrived at the junction with the ridge road, we could see large black clouds building up in the eastern sky. I hoped they weren't coming our way. It was now bitterly cold as we turned left and trotted the last half mile to the Lion Inn. I could see the red banners on the trailer and several other cars in the huge car park.

As we approached, we could hear strains of 'Congratulations' from the Brass band that was nestled in the lee of the Inn, trying to shelter from the cruel wind.

"Well done, Ann." My friend Joy rushed towards me, a big smile on her face and patted Danny-Boy. "Well done all of you," she called out, trying to make herself heard above the howling wind.

"Thanks. It's great to see you. I bet you're all frozen hanging around here." Al came over and Joe was there, too, to help with the horses. I asked Joe to hold Danny-Boy for me while I went to help Mick, who looked frozen.

"We'd better put Velvet and Cloey in the trailer," said Allan. I took Velvet from Mick, telling him to jump in the Land Rover until we'd sorted out the horses. After running the stirrups up while Allan let the tailgate down, I led her into the trailer. Sara followed with Cloey and after securing them with their lead reins, I fastened a hay-net up for them.

As I went to get Danny-Boy's sheet from the Land Rover the heavens opened and we were all pelted with hailstones! While Joe and I struggled to get the sheet on in the howling wind, Al went to help Maggie get Cammy's on. The horses didn't like the hailstones bouncing off them and swung round with their backs to the wind making our task more difficult. The sheets kept blowing up in the air, as we tried to fasten them.

Eventually, we had them both tethered to the trailer and gave them a small ration of food, by which time the shower had passed over.

"Phew, thank goodness for that," said Joe.

"Aye, just a bit rough, wasn't it," replied Allan. Sara collected the children from the shelter of the Land Rover and with Mick, we all walked across to the bar entrance where the band was still bravely playing. The wind was whipping up their music sheets and I'm sure their fingers must have been frozen. As we stopped to tell them how much we appreciated what they were doing, the sun suddenly broke through, so we stayed to listen to them for a while longer.

The Stape Brass Band had very kindly agreed to come and play during our lunch stop to attract the crowds. I had distributed posters locally, advertising their appearance. It was Bank Holiday weekend and we expected lots of people as this is a very well known area for hikers and day-trippers. I imagine the unseasonable weather had deterred some of them because it wasn't as busy as usual.

There were lots of familiar faces including Allan's brother Jack and sister-in-law Brenda. Joyce had returned, too, with some friends. Brenda and Joy had donned their tabards and were taking the collecting boxes round. Once inside, we ordered sandwiches and managed to find a vacant table where there was room for all the children, too. We had a lovely surprise when the landlord sent bowls of hot soup over for us all. We were all soon feeling a lot warmer as we sat near the open fire, drinking our soup.

All too soon it was time to brave the elements once more but when we went outside we were pleasantly surprised to see the day had improved. Mick had got warmed through and, feeling better after his rest, decided that he would ride across Rosedale with us. It didn't take us long with all our helpers to get the horses ready. Soon we were taking a track through the heather down on to the old disused railway line. This line runs right round the valley and was used to transport the iron ore that was mined in Rosedale for many years.

I have ridden on the line many times and it is one of my favourite rides. It's very quiet and beautiful up here in the head of the valley. Maggie also often rides round the line and we can look down to their farm as we circle the dale head. Riding over the old viaduct, I often wonder how they were built without all the heavy, powerful machinery available today. Parts of the way are a little tricky where the line has given way over the years but all the horses negotiated these places very well. Soon we were on the opposite side of the valley, climbing up a steep stony track through the heather away from the railway line.

Although there was a fresh breeze blowing when we reached the top of the hillside, it was pleasant riding as the sun kept breaking through the clouds and we had no more showers. Soon, we were back on the hard road and, waiting at the Fryup road junction, were Allan and Joyce. Mick again dismounted and let Joanne ride the last three miles down into Fryup. He looked very tired as he got into the car. He had done amazingly well to ride all that distance with us.

As we trotted down the road on our last stretch, Allan followed along behind us, which was just as well as it happened, because Cammy threw a shoe. Maggie was distraught.

"Don't worry, we'll put her in the trailer," I told her.

"Yes. But what about tomorrow? I really want to finish the ride with you," she faltered. I was looking at her crestfallen face and thinking hard at the same time. Maggie and I use the same blacksmith and Cammy was staying with us overnight.

"Don't worry. We'll ring David when we get home and, if the worst comes to the worst, Allan has been known to nail a shoe on in an emergency." She tried a weak smile. As Allan drew near, we explained to him what had happened. We soon had Cammy in the trailer and Maggie jumped in the Land Rover.

We left the road, taking a bridleway to the right across the moor and down a steep hillside track into Fryup Dale. Through the next gate and there was home! All the horses knew where we were and wanted to canter across the last field. As we reached the road near our house, there was a loud whinnying from the stable where Cammy was now tied up. She had heard us arrive and was certainly letting us know. The others answered her and the horses in my neighbour's field joined in too. The dogs were barking and the children were running round everywhere. It was quite a welcome!

The next half an hour was rather hectic. Chris had arrived with all the children to pick up Maggie. Mick and Joyce were there, too, to collect Joanne. After we untacked all the horses, Cloey was returned to the bottom field and Danny-Boy, Velvet and Cammy were all turned loose in the top field. There was much rolling, bucking around and high spirits as they enjoyed their freedom together. Back in the house it was coffee all round, after which Sara began to get the children ready for home.

"You look tired," I said when they came to say goodbye.

"Yes, I am a bit but I really enjoyed my ride and am glad that I was able to take part in it with you."

"Good. It was great having you along and I'm sure Cloey enjoyed it. You both did ever so well and she can rest tomorrow." I said goodbye to the grandchildren and off they went with Sara. Mick and Joyce left soon after as Mick needed to get home for a rest.

While Chris and Maggie drank their coffee, I tried to get through to

David, our farrier, on the phone but there was no answer. I left him a message and crossed my fingers. I reported back to Maggie and told her not to worry.

"We'll see you at the 'do' tonight and let you know how we've come on."

"Okay. We'd best get off now." We gave each other a big hug.

"Only one day to go. We're going to do it, you know," I told her confidently. She turned and followed Chris out of the door. "See you both later," I called after them. Now I had to think about the rest of the day.

The local hunts had organized a Sing-along evening over in the local at Rosedale to raise money for my cause. I went to find Al, who was starting to feed the dogs.

"Do you think I'd better run a raffle this evening?"

"Well, yes, I suppose so. Have you any prizes?"

"No, not really. I'd better pop to Castleton and buy some. We'll have tea when I get back." I dashed off, still in my jodhpurs and riding boots and came back with several prizes. After tea I went for my bath and washed my hair. It was all a bit of a rush, as it was soon time to get ready for church.

I received a lovely welcome from my fellow parishioners and lots of congratulations, including a public one from our priest. I felt like saying 'but I haven't finished it yet' and just hoped that I was going to. I said my thank you prayers for everything going so well so far. As I knelt and prayed, it didn't seem like a week since I was last there and that I had ridden all those miles. It was a bit sad really, to think that my long ride was almost over.

Back home, it was time to get ready for our evening out.

"I'll just go and check on the horses first," I told Al and went out to the field. Danny-Boy was laid out resting with Velvet standing nearby. Cammy was grazing a little further away, so I walked over to her. To my delight, I saw that she had a brand new set of shoes on. Good old David! He must have been while we were at church. Maggie would be thrilled.

Soon, for the second time that day, we were travelling back over the moor to Rosedale, armed with my prizes and raffle tickets. The place was almost full with friends and acquaintances. I gladly accepted my drink from Allan, as it had been a busy day and a drink was just what I needed! Shortly after, Mick arrived and I went across to speak with him.

"Hi, how are you feeling?"

"A bit tired but I had a sleep for an hour."

"You did really well today considering how cold it was," I told him. Allan walked over and joined us.

"Now Mick. How's things?"

"Not too bad but I won't stay too long. I want to try and ride a bit tomorrow if I'm all right."

"Well, we can put Velvet in the trailer and get her out when you're ready to ride," I suggested.

"Aye, okay. I'll be ovver in good time." The singing was getting under way, so it was a bit difficult to carry on a conversation. Presently, Maggie and Chris came in and made their way over to us. I smiled and moving closer to Maggie said,

"Guess what? Cammy's got four new shoes on." She beamed back at me.

"Honest? Oh, that's great news. I bet Allan's relieved." After Allan had bought their drinks, Maggie and I started to take our raffle tickets round. People were very generous and we sold many tickets. Everyone was having a great time and joining in all the singing. Some of the lads had travelled over from the Pennines especially to sing, which was really good of them. Later in the evening, we drew the raffle and shortly after this Mick came over to say goodnight. It was hard to realize that it was only yesterday that he'd been in hospital having treatment. Such courage made me feel very humble.

Throughout the evening, different people got up to sing and, as the night was drawing to a close, Dennis, the lad who'd organized the whole evening, came and asked me if I would sing. I was a bit taken aback and would rather not have.

"Come on Ann. These lads have come a long way to sing for you. They'll be disappointed if you don't sing for them." It was true. I had to pluck up courage and sing.

"Okay. But you all help me out if I forget the words." I told Dennis what I would sing. He asked for a bit of hush.

"Ann's going to sing a very special song for us." I needn't have worried. As soon as I started they all joined in with me and the whole room echoed to the sound of 'O Danny-Boy'. When I'd finished, I thanked Dennis and everyone else for making it such a successful evening and announced the amount of money we'd made. After we'd said goodnight to everyone, when Allan and I were walking back to the car, a young man approached me.

"How much money did you say you'd made tonight?" I knew his face as a hunting lad but not his name.

"Eighty pounds," I told him. He took my hand and put a twenty-pound note in it.

"I thought that's what you said. I'd like to make it up to a hundred for you. I think you've done a great job. Well done." I smiled and thanked him, overcome by his generosity. He said goodnight and was gone.

I got in the car with Allan and on the way home recalled in my mind all that had happened that day. It had been a long one and now I had only one day left of my big adventure.

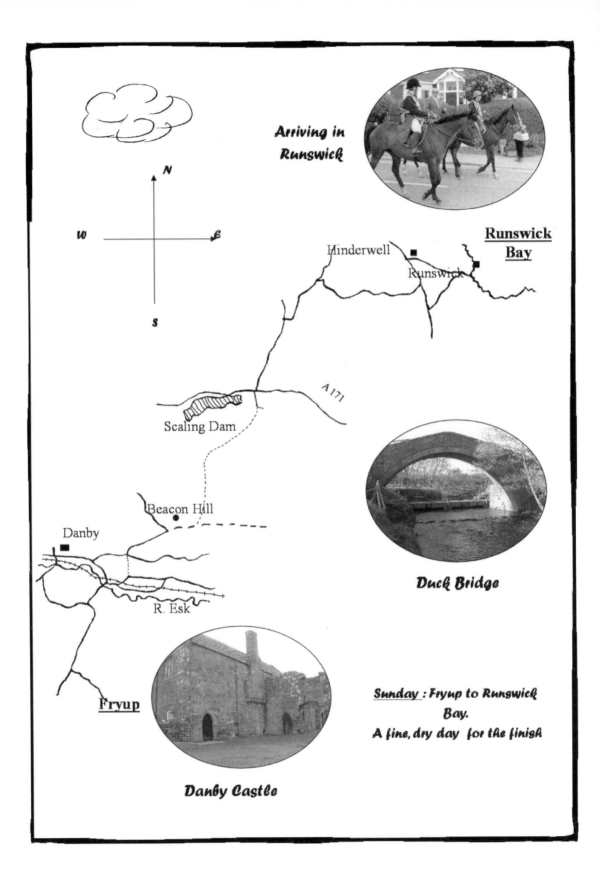

Arriving in
Runswick

N

W   E

S

Runswick
Bay

Hinderwell

Runswick

A 171

Scaling Dam

Duck Bridge

Beacon Hill

Danby

R. Esk

Fryup

Sunday : Fryup to Runswick
Bay.
A fine, dry day for the finish

Danby Castle

SUNDAY MAY 28

FRYUP TO

RUNSWICK BAY

My last day. I could scarcely believe how quickly the week had passed. The barking of the dogs told me I should be up. For once it wasn't raining and after a hurried breakfast I went to bring the horses in.

I called out to them as I walked round to the stable with a bucketful of hand food. Velvet whinnied loudly and came trotting down the field, with Danny-Boy following close behind. Cammy paused in her grazing, lifted her head and decided that she, too, had better follow. She slowly made her way down the field after the others. I soon had them tied up and eating their hand food. Apart from a bit of mud on their legs, they weren't too bad and wouldn't take a lot of grooming. I returned to the house to make the coffee.

"Well, it's nice to have a dry morning, Al."

"Aye, should stay dry all day, according to the forecast. What time are you setting off this morning?"

"Ten o'clock. We should be able to do it in about four hours." This was going to be the shortest day's ride of the week.

"Have you put fresh water in for the horses?" I asked.

"Not yet. I'm going to do it next while you're getting the horses brushed. Do you think we ought to take some hay nets?"

"Mm, might be a good idea. I don't know how long they'll be in the trailer when we've finished." After coffee, I went to groom the horses. I was returning to the house for Danny-Boy's saddle, when I heard a vehicle pull up. It was Mick.

"Hi, how are you this morning?"

"A bit stiff but not too bad."

"Good. Come on in and have a drink, while I see to the horses."

"Thanks. You'll be tacking Velvet up ready?"

"Yes. I was just starting when you arrived." I was handing Mick his coffee when Allan came in. "I expect you'll be wanting another now?" I grinned at him.

"Aye. Good idea." I was soon back in the stable and busy with Danny-Boy, when suddenly Maggie appeared in the doorway.

"Morning," she greeted me with her usual big smile.

"Hi, I didn't hear you arrive. Everyone all right?" I asked.

"Yes, fine thanks. Horses look okay?"

"Yeah, grand." She placed her saddle over the stable door and set to with a brush on Cammy. I soon had the saddles and bridles on

Velvet and Danny-Boy and returned to the house to get washed and changed into my jodhpurs. Chris, who had brought Maggie over, was sitting inside, chatting with the other two.

Twenty minutes later, we had Velvet loaded into the trailer and Maggie and I were mounted up ready to start our final day. Although a bit dull, it was fine and dry as we set off at a trot down the road. I was sure Danny-Boy was wondering why we were off again, having just travelled all that way to get home!

We made our way along Little Fryup dale, past Danby Castle and down the narrow lane to Duck Bridge. This is where the new raised ford was built to save wear and tear on the old historic bridge. It is where Dan drowned and it's only natural that I think of him every time I have to cross the river that claimed his life. He was such a happy, carefree character, always willing to please. I had been very blessed to be given such a son as Dan. My horse was well named.

We turned right on the Lealholm to Danby road and almost immediately turned left under the railway bridge up a narrow farm lane. At the top of the hill we again turned left up a Green lane with stone walls on either side. Once through the gate at the top, we were out on the moor, taking the road to the well known site of Danby Beacon. This is the highest point on these low moors and you can see for miles. Although no longer standing, the seven beacons that used to be there are well remembered. We could see them from the farm where I lived as a child. It is a popular place for hikers and tourists who like to walk their dogs along the moor edges, but this morning it was very quiet and deserted.

From the 'Beacon' we had to ride down an old rough road for a short way until we reached the bridleway on our left down Brown Rigg. Riding down here we could see far across the moor to the farms, and beyond that, the grey waters of the North Sea.

"Is that Scaling Dam?" enquired Maggie, pointing to the large expanse of water, way down the moor to our left.

"Yes. It looks lovely when the sun's shining and all the different coloured sailing boats are out. There is a lot of wildlife on and around the water, too, as it is a nature reserve."

"Do you go down there much?"

"Only if I'm riding nearby. There is a hide down by the water and Allan and I keep saying that we must go with the cameras sometime but that day hasn't come yet."

"I know what you mean." She sighed wistfully. "There never seems to be time to do things like that." We trotted on down the moor, the heather dull and brown, its new green shoots still many weeks away. We passed a row of shooting butts that blended in to their surroundings with their expert covering of heather and bilberry patches. There were beds of seves, soft boggy areas covered in varying shades of green, spongy mosses and occasional patches of dead, golden bracken. It was very peaceful, the silence only broken by the harsh call of the grouse as we startled them.

Eventually, we reached the rough farm track that would lead us down to the main Whitby road. I knew the traffic would be heavy, as it always is on a Sunday, with people making their way to the coast for the day. I could see the Land Rover parked on the by-road on the far side and as we neared the main road, I noticed Mick standing by the gate, waiting to open it for us.

We had to wait quite a while until it was safe for us to cross the road, then we trotted quickly to the other side.

"We'll wait for you down near Borrowby," said Mick, as he climbed back into the Land Rover. "Then I'll try and ride the rest of the way."

"Okay," I called, as they set off down the road. The horses were calling to each other as we followed on behind.

"I thought he'd be shattered after yesterday," commented Maggie.

"He probably is," I replied, "but he won't give in. He's set his heart on doing it."

"I think he's marvellous. A wonderful example to all of us." We trotted on past farms and cottages, the sea getting ever closer. We continued on for a couple of miles until we reached the narrow lane on our right, which would take us through the fields to Hinderwell. Allan was dropping the tailgate of the trailer and Velvet soon started shouting when she heard the clip-clop of hooves on the road. She backed out of the trailer in a hurry, frightened that we would go without her. Allan held her while Mick let down the stirrups and pulled himself up into the saddle. He gathered up the reins and soon had Velvet settled down.

"Right, lasses, I'm ready."

"Okay, we'll be off then. See you in Runswick, Al." I turned and waved as we set off down the hill on the narrow lane. There were leafy hedgerows on either side with a strong scent of May blossom in the air. We passed fields of sheep with their lambs, and cows lying contentedly chewing their cud. Only the sound of birds whistling and singing could be heard above the clatter of hooves as we rode along. We trotted for short distances but walked for long spells, as I could see that Mick was tiring. We had plenty of time.

We chatted and talked together, telling Mick about our ride. Maggie's infectious laughter would ring out across the still countryside, as we remembered some of the amusing incidents. I had mixed feelings as we rode along. I felt excitement at the thought of what we had almost accomplished and sadness because my great adventure was almost over. The time went quickly and all too soon we were coming out on to the main road near Hinderwell. The traffic was quite heavy but we were all right, as there was a large grass verge alongside the road and we even had a little canter before we reached the village.

We turned right in the village and walked the last mile down to Runswick Bay. My heart was pounding with elation and I looked across at Maggie, her cheeks flushed with pleasure.

"We're really going to do it, Ann," she said, beaming across at me. I could sense the excitement in her voice.

"Of course we are. There's less than a mile to go," I replied, smiling back at her. Cars were passing by us, their occupants waving. As we got nearer to the hotel and the car park opposite, we could see lots of people milling around. We rode three abreast, with Mick between Maggie and myself, and were greeted with loud cheers and hand clapping. I can't describe how I felt. It seemed so unreal, like a dream. Was this really happening? Had I ridden all those miles? Every inch of the way? I didn't know whether to cry with happiness or shout for joy. I felt very emotional as I lay forward onto Danny-Boy's neck and patted him.

"We did it Danny-Boy. We really did it." Allan came over and squeezed my hand. The smile on his face said it all. I knew he was both proud of and pleased for me.

"Well done, mate," was all he said. Suddenly there seemed to be people everywhere. Maggie's family were all around, patting Cammy and shouting, excitedly. Our son Dave was there and Allan's brother and his wife. Suddenly, my young brother Jimmy was reaching up to give me a hug, a huge, lopsided grin on his face.

"Congratulations, Sis. Always knew you would do it," he said. I seemed to be in a daze with a permanent grin on my face.

"I can't believe I'm here. It's great to see you all. Didn't Danny-Boy do well?" I couldn't stop patting him and pulling gently on his ears. I'm sure he knew what a tremendous moment this was and I was so proud of him. Someone exclaimed how well he looked. Maybe they expected he would look a little leaner and tired but he was in great shape. He appeared to be enjoying all the attention that he was receiving, as different people kept coming over to talk to us. Kathy was there taking pictures, delighted that we had completed our journey. Then I heard a familiar voice behind and turning, was delighted to see our elder son, Mike beaming up at me.

"Well done, Patty." This is his pet name for me. He was dressed in his work clothes. I leaned down to embrace him.

"Hi, I'm so glad you've come. I wasn't expecting to see you. You look as if you've been busy?"

"Yes. I'm on a job a few miles away, so took a late lunch break to pop over and see you." He walked round to the front of Danny-Boy, patting his neck as he did so. "He looks well, doesn't he?"

"Yeah, he's been great. The week went really well."

"Good. I'll just have a word with Dad, and then I'll have to get back to work. I'll be up to see you both soon and you can tell me all about it." He gave me his usual cheeky grin, winked at me and went to find his Dad.

The landlord of the hotel had been out to welcome us all. This was the very same man, who, all those years before, had let me ride his pony, Misty. Dick had changed his occupation and now, with his new partner, Anne, ran a very successful hotel. He had been only too glad to hold our celebration party at his premises. He had been chatting to Mick, whom he knew from his days on the farm in Rosedale.

Presently, he went back inside and returned with two glasses of champagne. Maggie and I happily accepted them and, while still on horseback, with one arm round each other, we raised our glasses to a rousing cheer.

"And here's to Danny-Boy and Cammy," I whispered to Maggie. She squeezed my shoulder and smiled. We both knew who the real heroes had been.

Mick, with Allan's help, had already unsaddled Velvet and she was now munching on her hay in the trailer. I knew it was time to put

Danny-Boy in too, but was reluctant for this special time to end. I knew it was a moment of a lifetime and I wanted it to go on forever. Once I dismounted, that would be it, the end of my great adventure. We did eventually, with some reluctance, dismount and untack our horses and put them in their trailers. Danny-Boy went in with Velvet and Cammy went in her own trailer, which Chris had brought over with him. We took off our hats and, for the last time, removed our distinctive red tabards before joining everyone in the bar for more celebratory drinks.

A local country music artist had agreed to come and entertain us and everyone was enjoying the music, singing along and dancing. Kathy came over to meet us as Maggie and I entered.

"Come with me a minute. I've got a surprise for you." We followed her through the bar and into the dining room beyond. There, on one of the tables, was a beautiful decorated cake, iced with the figure of a horse's head and the words 'Well Done.'

"Oh, Kathy, that's absolutely lovely," exclaimed Maggie. I was so surprised and overcome with emotion that I just put my arm around Kathy and said,

"It's beautiful. Thanks Kathy, for everything."

"No, it's me that should be thanking both of you. You've done marvellous." I told Kathy how much money we'd collected so far before we all returned to the bar. Kathy carried the cake through so that we could cut it in front of everyone. I persuaded Mick to stand with us while Maggie and I prepared to cut the cake.

Kathy stood up to make a small speech. She spoke of her

appreciation for our venture and added that the weather hadn't always been brilliant.

"I have been on holiday this past week, so know the amount of discomfort they had to endure. Ann tells me that she knows that she has so far raised £2,800 and this total will increase when she has

collected all the sponsor sheets in, which is wonderful." This was met with much applause and then we cut the cake, whereupon Kathy led the singing of 'For She's a jolly Good Fellow.' Mick was finding this all a bit too much and was having difficulty keeping the tears back. I put my hand on his shoulder and told him he was doing great, before he made his way back to his wife.

The singing started once more and there was much laughter and talking as Maggie and I replied to the various questions about our big ride. Everyone seemed to be infected by the sheer joy and jubilation that Maggie and I were feeling. The cake, which had now been cut up, was handed round to everyone present.

I was approaching the bar when Dick called me over, saying how great it was seeing Mick again.

"He's been amazing, hasn't he? I'll never forget the day I went hunting with him on that pony, Misty. I hadn't been riding very long and we were going down a rough sheep track at Hangman's Slack and the bracken was shoulder high. Suddenly, Misty fell in a hole and sent me flying over her head into the bracken. When I picked myself up, she was nowhere to be seen. I don't know who I cussed most, myself or Misty." Dick chuckled as he continued his story. "I was thinking that it was a hell of a walk home, if that's where she'd gone. I struggled down the hill and came out into a clearing and there was Mick leading my pony. 'Is this your 'oss, Dick?' he asked me, a twinkle in his eye." Dick laughed as he continued and I smiled as I pictured the scene he described. "By, was I glad to see him. I had some great days with Mick. Wonderful bloke to ride with." Still chuckling over his memories, he turned to serve another customer.

Kathy had to leave early and came over to say goodbye. I promised to get in touch and arrange to meet her when all the money was collected in. Some others had left for home, too, but those who remained were in a party mood and started dancing. Maggie and I joined in, singing along to the music as we danced.

"It's the first time I've ever danced in my riding boots," I said.

"I would still be dancing even if I was wearing hob-nailed boots," she replied, laughing. Happiness was bubbling from her like a mountain stream. "I still can't believe we really did it."

"Me neither. It all seems so unreal."

As if to endorse our ecstatic feelings of joy, the final song played was 'It's a Beautiful Day.' We danced through to the end, finishing with a huge hug for one another.

"I'm so glad you came with me. I couldn't have had a better companion to ride along with."

"Thanks. I'm so glad I was able to come with you. It's been marvellous."

Most people were getting ready to leave. Maggie was collecting up her family ready for home. I went to thank our entertainer for all his hard work, then went to find our hosts. Dick gave me the sponsor sheet, which had been displayed in the bar and all the money he'd collected.

"Thank you both very much for today. It's been wonderful. I'll let you know what the final total is, when it's all gathered in."

"Hang on a minute Annie." He always calls me that to tease me because he knows I don't like it. He disappeared round the back of the bar and, on returning, placed a roll of notes into my hand.

"Put that into your collection, too. You've done a great job."

"Thanks, Dick. That's more than generous," I smiled at him. "We'll be back to see you soon." I gathered up the collecting boxes that my friends, Baz and Margaret from the choir, had enthusiastically been putting to good use. These I gave to Al while I went to collect the remains of my cake.

As we went outside, Chris and Maggie, with their children, were pulling out of the car park. They all waved madly when they saw us.

"See you soon," I shouted as we waved back to them. It was a poignant moment, as I knew then that our great adventure was finally over. I started to cross the road and suddenly noticed Mick, leaning on some railings, gazing out to sea. As I walked over to him, a lump came to my throat, wondering what were his thoughts. Would this be the last time he would watch the waves breaking over the golden sands? How much longer would he be able to ride his beautiful mare, Velvet?

"Come on Mick." I put my arm round his shoulder. "It's home time."

"Aye, I'se about tired." He managed a weak smile as we turned and walked back to the Land Rover, where Al was waiting for us.

When we arrived back at Fryup, I helped load Velvet into Mick's trailer that he had brought with him in the morning. I waved him goodbye before getting Danny-Boy from the trailer and leading him round to his stable. I talked to him as I removed his sheet.

"Well, that's it, old fella. The end of our big ride. I hope you enjoyed it as much as I did." I patted his neck and stroked his face, as he rested his muzzle on my shoulder. I could feel his warm breath on my face and take in that wonderful horsey smell. I sighed, momentarily, before straightening and saying cheerfully, "There's always tomorrow. Who knows what the future holds." I led him from the stable and turned him loose in the field, saying, "Go and relax, enjoy your freedom. You've certainly earned it."

REFLECTIONS

AND

REALITIES

Life slowly returned to normal as I tried to get back into a regular routine again. I found it hard accepting that I had really finished my ride that had taken me so long to plan. The week had passed far too quickly and I felt I wanted to do it all again, without all the commitment and pressures. As I went about my daily jobs, I relived many of the moments on my ride. Watching Danny-Boy relaxing in his field made me feel very proud of what we had achieved.

I had plenty to do to keep me busy, for besides all the usual household chores, the never-ending upkeep of the garden and kennels, I was revisiting all the people and places where I had delivered sponsorship forms and posters. I was pleasantly surprised by the amount that I was collecting, and the total was growing in my special bank account. There were still letters arriving daily in the post with more donations, which was great.

I arranged a meeting with Carol and Ian to organize some letters and posters. Ian volunteered to draft a poster thanking all those who had sponsored me and stating the total money raised. Carol typed up many thankyou letters for all those who had sent postal donations. I wrote letters of thanks to Richard Burridge, to our local country artist who had entertained us at Runswick Bay and to the Stape Brass band. Later, when all the money had been collected, I wrote to David and Marie, Mr. Jackson, the reporter, cousin Pete, Laurie and Linda and to Mary.

I was also trying to arrange a presentation evening. My friend Sharon (who manages a licensed restaurant in the village) agreed to hold a domino drive, after which I could present the cheque for all the money raised to the L.R.F. representative. Trying to fix a date for this was rather difficult, as there was always someone who couldn't make it on a certain night.

Eventually, a date was fixed for late June and I asked my neighbour Brian to design and print some posters. I started collecting prizes and contacted the local *Gazette*, and I got in touch with Kathy, who contacted the Leukaemia Research representative from Head Office, Jennifer Baxter. Jennifer gladly accepted the invitation to attend our presentation evening, saying how good it would be to visit somewhere in the countryside for a change.

As the evening of the domino drive drew closer, I was becoming increasingly more nervous. I knew that I would have to make a small speech. Not something that I was accustomed to doing. The night arrived and a good crowd turned out. The *Gazette* sent a reporter and a photographer. Maggie and Chris came over from Rosedale for the evening and, much to my delight, Mary arrived and agreed to stay overnight with us. Mick managed to come, although he was looking very tired and pale, as he had once more been receiving treatment. Ian was chairing the evening for me and as usual, Joe ran the dominoes and announced the raffle and prize winners.

Inevitably the time came for me to stand up and say my piece. I had made a list of all the many people that I had to thank, because I knew I wouldn't possibly be able to remember everyone. When Ian introduced me, I stood up, my knees shaking, and smiled at the room full of expectant faces.

"First, thank you all for coming here this evening and sharing in this presentation. I have had such marvellous support from so many people but there are a few I must thank in person. I hope that I don't miss anyone out. Ian, for all his help in our planning of the ride and Carol for all the hours she spent typing out dozens of letters. My brother Tony and his wife Stella for looking after all our animals while we were away. Nick and Charlotte, for the loan of the trailer. Joe and Carol, again, for the wonderful support they gave us at the beginning of the week. My excellent companion Maggie, with her horse Cammy, for accompanying me on my ride. I couldn't have wished for anyone better with whom to share my great adventure. Not only for her company while riding, but also for her vivacity and high spirits in the evenings, especially when she sampled the Jack Daniels." This was received with much amusement.

"I am very grateful to my farrier, David, who shod both our horses free of charge for our week's ride. He was confident that the shoes would last out the week. They almost did, didn't they Maggie? On the Saturday afternoon with one day to go, Cammy threw a shoe. I was unable to contact David so keeping my fingers crossed that he would pick up the phone, I left him a message. He came and replaced the shoe while we were at church, enabling Maggie to complete the ride with me."

"There were many people who took sponsor sheets or displayed them in their establishments but I must thank my youngest helper, Anne-Marie. Although only twelve years old she managed to raise over eighty pounds on her sponsor sheet. An excellent effort. I have great admiration and appreciation for all those who worked so hard with the collecting boxes during our ride. Never an easy task and the weather wasn't always brilliant for them either. Thank you all very much." I looked across to where Kathy was standing.

"Kathy, I really appreciate all the guidance and support you always give me in my fund-raising efforts. Many thanks go to Sharon and her parents for making us all so welcome this evening and providing such a lovely supper. And, last but not least, the biggest thanks of all, goes to my long suffering husband, Allan, without whom none of this would have been possible. He was always there, filling water buckets, collecting sheets and lead ropes, piling everything into the Land Rover and cleaning up after us. Al, you did a great job. Thank you very much. Thank you *all* very much." I smiled gratefully at their applause, sat down thankfully, relieved that I had managed okay.

Ian next introduced Jennifer, who spoke about where the money we'd raised would go, and how it would be used. Also how important it is to keep funding the research, as great strides are being made in the treatment of Leukaemia. She was most appreciative of *all* our efforts, knowing that I couldn't have raised such a huge amount on my own. Next, Kathy presented me with a large bouquet of flowers and a certificate of appreciation signed by the chief executive, no less! She also had certificates for Ian, Carol and Maggie, adding what a tremendous amount of hard work had gone into, not only the ride, but in all the preparations beforehand.

After thanking Jennifer and Kathy, Ian continued.

"I am now going to ask Ann and Maggie to present their cheque to Kathy who will accept it on behalf of the Leukaemia Research Fund." Maggie and I took hold of the especially large cheque that had been issued to me from my bank.

"Ann has raised the grand total of £5,750. A magnificent achievement." There were a few gasps of amazement as well as a spontaneous applause when Maggie and I handed the cheque to a beaming Kathy. It was a lovely end to a wonderful evening.

It's a good job we don't always know what life has in store for us. A few weeks after our presentation evening, Sharon and I were going on an early morning ride through the hills. It's often the best time to ride during the summer months to avoid the flies. Also it suits Sharon as she starts work at ten o'clock. It was a lovely morning and we were riding through the hills in Fryup Head. I was riding Cloey and Sharon was on Danny-Boy. We approached a stone bridge over a small stream and as it was soft either side of the stone due to recent heavy rain, Danny-Boy elected to jump the stream a little to the right. I saw him catch his right, hind foot on the corner of a stone as he jumped and was walking a little gingerly on it. We continued on the path through the bracken.

"Is he all right?" Sharon asked, referring to Danny-Boy. "He feels quite lame." I was following behind them on Cloey.

""Well, he's certainly favouring his back leg. He's probably numbed it. I expect it will wear off."

"Did you see what happened?"

"Yes. He just caught his back foot on the corner of a stone. It was a bit careless of him, really. We'll walk a bit further and see if it wears off." Soon we reached a small gate and after opening it, while I was dismounted, I had a look at the affected foot. There was a small trickle of blood just above the coronet band but it didn't look very serious. Sharon looked concerned.

"I don't feel I ought to ride him, Ann."

"You ride Cloey a while and I'll ride Danny-Boy," I ventured. We swapped horses and continued walking down the grassy track leading to the fields. I could feel the foot was bothering him and the lameness wasn't wearing off as I'd hoped it would. I again dismounted to open another gate into the fields.

"I'll lead him down to the road and see if it improves." By the time we'd travelled down the two fields to the road, the lameness was getting progressively worse. I was beginning to feel quite worried. Danny-Boy was practically carrying the offending leg. I opened the last gate on to the road and knew then that the injury was serious.

Danny-Boy wouldn't put any weight on the injured limb once we were on the hard road. The dogs started barking at the farm on the opposite side of the road and Frank, a good friend and neighbour came out to see us. I didn't like the expression on his face. Frank had ridden all his life and kept a pony for shepherding on the moors, so knew enough about horses to recognise that I had a big problem.

"You've got a very lame horse there, Ann. What happened? Are *you* all right?" he queried. I explained how the injury had occurred.

"We'd best try and get him into my field. I don't think he can walk far on that leg."

"No, he can't," I agreed. "It's getting worse by the minute." Sharon was looking on, a grave expression on her face. I thought she was going to burst into tears.

"I'm sorry Ann," she half whispered in a shaky voice.

"It's okay Shar, it wasn't your fault at all. You take Cloey home or you'll be late for work." I tried to smile to make her feel better. "Frank will run me home and I'll let you know how we come on." She agreed to go and set off down the road, her shoulders sagging and head bowed. I knew that she was blaming herself for the mishap. With a great deal of tugging and persuading, Frank and I eventually persuaded Danny-Boy to hobble across the road and into the field. He was obviously in a lot of pain and he whinnied loudly as he saw Cloey trotting off down the road without him. I removed his saddle and bridle, talking gently to him as I did so. My throat felt constricted and I was close to tears.

"I'll be back soon, old fella. I've got to go and get help for you." I patted his neck and turned away, carrying his tack across to Frank's Land Rover. Frank could see I was upset as we travelled the mile or so back home.

"Don't worry about getting him home yet until the vet's seen him. He'll be all right in my field."

"Thanks," was all I could manage in reply.

Once back home, I contacted the vet and described what had happened. They promised to have someone out by one o'clock to examine him, adding that it might be necessary to take x-rays to discover the extent of the injury. I felt sick inside, worrying about Danny-Boy and hoping against hope that he hadn't broken anything. I tried contacting Allan on his mobile but couldn't find him. I set off in the car to look for him knowing roughly where he might be working. I found the other two keepers up on the high moors, repairing the shooting butts for the coming season, but they didn't know where Allan was. They were, however, meeting up at lunchtime, so I asked them to pass a message on to him for me.

I returned home and waited. I couldn't concentrate on anything and as lunchtime approached I became more anxious and certainly couldn't eat anything. I hoped Al would return before it was time for the vet's arrival. I was sitting on the settee, shaking with fear, thinking of what I might have to face with Danny-Boy. Surely, horses had to be put down if they broke a leg? I couldn't bear to think of it. Suddenly, I heard the Land Rover pull up outside and Allan came rushing in.

"The lads said you'd had an accident. Are you all right?" I nodded and burst into tears.

"It's not me," I sobbed. "It's Danny-Boy." He came and sat down beside me, putting his arm round my shoulder.

"It can't be that bad. Where is he? What happened?" I tried between my sobs to tell him what had taken place.

"I think it might be broken," I finished desperately.

" I'll just go and sort the lads out, then I'll come up to Frank's with you."

Half an hour later we were pulling up in Frank's yard. Danny-Boy had hardly moved from where I'd left him. I went into the field to see him while Allan stayed and talked to Frank. Soon after, the vet arrived and came over to me. Again I relayed my story while he examined Danny-Boy. I waited anxiously for his diagnosis.

"Well, he's certainly in a lot of pain. It could be just badly bruised but there's no way of telling until we take some x-rays." We walked back up to the yard and he explained the situation to Allan and Frank.

"Would it be possible to do them here?" he asked Frank, referring to the x-rays.

"By all means. There's a power point in this building," he replied, pointing to a door. While Frank assisted the vet to set up all the equipment, Allan and I took the lead rope and head collar and went to try and persuade Danny-Boy to walk up from the field on to the cement driveway. Poor old boy, he struggled on three legs as we eventually got him in a suitable position. After taking several plates, the vet packed away his gear and promised to ring me with the results around five o'clock. We led Danny-Boy back to the field and after telling Frank I'd be in touch, went home to wait.

The afternoon dragged by as I anxiously awaited the results. When eventually the phone did ring, I was almost too scared to answer it. The vet's voice came over the phone. I could feel my heart pounding inside me.

"Sorry I've taken so long but I had another callout. I've got the results of the x-rays. The news is both bad and good." My hopes were lifted momentarily. He continued. "The bad news is that the foot is broken." I'm sure he must have heard my gasp of despair down the phone. "The good news is that if you're going to break a bone, break one in the foot. The hoof acts as a natural cast." He went on to explain what the procedure would be and the chances of Danny-Boy becoming sound again. No mention of the possibility that he may have to be put down. I asked him what I had to do with Danny-Boy.

The vet was going to return six days later when some of the internal inflammation would have subsided. I had to arrange for the farrier to be present when the vet returned, as the shoe would have to be removed, in order to take more x-rays from a different angle. After this, a special shoe would have to be fitted. The vet went on to explain that the stone on which Danny-boy had caught his foot, had acted like an axe on a log, catching the top and splitting the bone from top to bottom.

"Don't worry too much," he said. "It looks like a very clean break with no misalignment. We'll know more when we see the next lot of x-rays. In the meantime, get him back home and keep him stalled in his stable." I hung up, feeling numb inside. Would he ever be sound again? Once more, I couldn't hold back the tears.

I could hardly take in what had happened. It seemed so unfair that Danny-Boy had carried me all those miles across the breadth of England, never getting a scratch and yet here he was with a broken foot, just riding round such familiar territory. I was devastated. It seemed so cruel, especially after he had raised all that money. I went to bed that night with a heavy heart, unable to control my tears, wondering if I would ever ride my beloved Danny-Boy again.

The next morning I awoke with a feeling of dread, knowing the task ahead was not going to be easy. After our usual jobs, Allan and I hitched up the trailer and set off back to Frank's. Allan drove the Land Rover right down the field to where Danny-Boy was standing, still holding his hind leg off the ground. We lowered the tailgate and after putting on his halter, tried to walk him up the ramp.

Allan held the lead rope and, with Frank's help, I tried to persuade Danny-Boy to walk in. He stepped on to the ramp with his front legs but that was it. He just didn't know how to walk in with only one hind leg. I have never felt so cruel as I did that day. As Allan pulled on his lead rope, I tried to encourage Danny-Boy into the trailer. I forcibly lifted his front feet, one at a time, further up the ramp and then ended up having to use my crop on his rump to force him to hop on to the tailgate. After a series of manoeuvres and a lot of persuading, we finally managed to get him inside. I was so upset that I stayed in the trailer with him and tried to console him while we travelled the short distance home.

Getting Danny-Boy out of the trailer proved to be almost as

difficult as getting him in. Allan drove the Land Rover into the field, which slopes down towards the stable, so that when we lowered the tailgate it would be almost level with the ground. If Danny-Boy had found it difficult hopping into the trailer, he found it much more difficult trying to hop out backwards. Eventually, we had him on the grass and I slowly led him down into his stable and treated him to some hand food. I clipped him into his stall and laid a deep bed of straw down for him. I wished that there was something more that I could do for him.

Six days later, while David was removing the shoe from the injured foot, the vet arrived. He took several more x-rays from different angles and then David fitted the specially forged shoe that he had made. The vet told me that Danny-Boy could now go outside into a small paddock. After that it would be a long wait and all I could do was hope and pray.

In the weeks that followed, I became used to seeing Danny-Boy hobbling about the field. Some days he just couldn't resist having a canter but he soon learned how painful that was to him and managed to curtail his enthusiasm. As time went on, the hobble became more of a limp and eventually was only recognisable when he trotted.

After three months, the special shoe was refitted and after a further three months, I was able to start walking him out gently. During these months, having Cloey to ride was a great help to me. It helped to relieve some of the frustration and sadness that I felt.

Christmas came and went. In January Mick finally decided that riding Velvet had become too much of a struggle for him. As it

happened, within a couple of weeks, no-one was riding anywhere because everywhere was prohibited due to the awful outbreaks of Foot and Mouth disease. As a result of this, Danny-Boy endured a much longer lay-off than was anticipated. I suppose in the long run, this was no bad thing, as it gave his foot much longer to heal.

During the summer, I advertised Velvet for sale and had the difficult task of finding a new home for her. It was a very sad time as I loved to ride her over the moors and I knew that she would never again come to stay with us. It was doubly sad for Mick having to part with his beautiful mare, of whom he was so proud. The only consolation was that she eventually went to a very good home, where a huntsman was going to ride her to hounds. His wife and daughter, who both loved horses, would be caring for her and also riding out on her. It was August when we loaded Velvet into the trailer and she went off to her new home.

In September, the surgeon who was attending Mick at the hospital decided to cease all his treatment. He had become so ill that it was having only an adverse affect on him. His sight and hearing were failing and he was growing very weak. It was with great sadness that we witnessed his losing battle against the illness that he had so bravely fought for over eight years. In December, with his wife and all his family gathered round his bedside, he lost his long battle and passed peacefully into a new pain-free afterlife.

The New Year brought new hope to the countryside and things slowly got back to normal. Farmers, including one of my brothers, who had lost everything, were able to restock. The beautiful countryside in which we live was once again open to horses and people alike.

Once more I could ride over the moors that I love and reflect on the happenings of life. There have been disappointments and much heartache but life can be very rewarding, too. I am more than grateful that Danny-Boy has made a complete recovery but sad that we lost a very dear friend in Mick, who will ride these wild and rugged moors no more. I think of his amazing courage and bravery that inspired me to raise thousands of pounds for the fight against Leukaemia.

I think often of Dan and the chasm he left in our lives that nothing can ever fill. I think too, of that special week in my life, when I rode across the country on Danny-Boy with Maggie and Cammy, enabling me to fulfil a lifelong dream.

Everyone has their dreams. Yet despite all the heartaches and dis-appointments in life, if you have hope in the future, dreams can come true. My dream became a reality and the memories of that reality will remain with me forever.

THE END